Penguin Education

Penguin Education Specials
General Editor: Willem van der Eyken

D1076541

Letter to a Teacher
By the School of Barbiana

Letter to a Teacher

By the School of Barbiana

Translated by Nora Rossi and Tom Cole

With an Afterword by Lord Boyle of Handsworth

Penguin Books

Penguin Books Ltd, Harmondsworth,
Middlesex, England
Penguin Books Australia Ltd,
Ringwood, Victoria, Australia

This translation first published in the U.S.A.
by Random House 1970
First published in Great Britain by Penguin Books 1970
Copyright © School of Barbiana, 1969
This translation copyright © Random House, Inc., 1970

Made and printed in Great Britain by
Hazell Watson & Viney Ltd,
Aylesbury, Bucks
Set in Linotype Plantin

This book is not written for teachers, but for parents. It is a call for them to organize.

At first sight it seems written by one boy alone. Actually we, the authors, are eight boys from the school of Barbiana.

Other schoolmates, who are now at work, helped us on Sundays.

We want to give thanks first of all to Father Milani, who trained us, taught us the rules of writing and supervised our work.

In the second place, a great many friends who co-operated in different ways:
Parents, who helped us to simplify the text.
Secretaries, teachers, supervisors, school principals, officers of the Ministry of Education and of ISTAT,* priests, all of whom helped us to collect statistical data.
Union officials, newspaper men, civic administrators, historians, statisticians, jurists, who provided us with various kinds of information.

* ISTAT: Istituto Centrale di Statistiche (Central Institute of Statistics) [Translators' note].

Contents

Translators' Introduction

Barbiana is not the name of a school nor the name of a town. It is a community of about twenty farmhouses in the hills of the Mugello region, in Tuscany. The church of Barbiana, a small, lovely building of the fourteenth century, stands on a hill overlooking the valley. It is reached by a winding dirt road from Vicchio. Vicchio, known as the birthplace of Giotto, is located about thirty miles from Florence on a road branching off from the old highway that connects Florence to Bologna through the Apennines.

The landscape has a harsh beauty: woods, stony slopes and a few scattered fields and orchards.

Don Lorenzo Milani, founder of the school of Barbiana, was ordered to the Barbiana church in 1954. He went there from Calenzano, a town near Florence, where as a young priest he had started a night school for the working people. The school soon attracted those who found in its classes, tailored to their needs, the encouragement or inspiration to pursue their interests or go on with their studies.

Soon after being ordered to Barbiana, Lorenzo Milani felt the needs of the children of the farms scattered near by to be very critical. Most of the children had either failed their exams and left school or were bitterly discouraged with the way they were taught. He gathered about ten boys, eleven to thirteen year olds, and gave them a full timetable of eight hours' work, six or seven days a week. Later, the group grew to twenty. The older children would devote a great deal of time to teaching or drilling the younger. Many hours were given by all to the study and understanding of problems directly significant to their own lives, and, along these lines, eight students of the school wrote this *Letter* as a full-year project.

Don Lorenzo Milani died in the summer of 1967, and the school at Barbiana died with him. And yet it is still alive. With the magnetizing strength of their priest gone, a number of the farmers followed the inevitable trend of migration to the valley or to Florence. But their children have not lost contact with one another or with the little church. They all work: some in the trade unions, some in factories or as technicians; others are studying to become teachers. Often on Sundays they get together in the old classroom to discuss things.

When one of the translators visited Barbiana in the summer of 1968, a group from an orphanage in Florence was camped there, and some of the 'old' Barbiana students – now aged sixteen or seventeen – were teaching the younger children. Gathered around rickety tables, under the trellises, in the kitchen – children of all ages were hard at work everywhere. In the autumn, the school of Barbiana officially moved to Calenzano, where some of the former Barbiana students, together with old friends and other pupils of Don Milani, have opened a regular *doposcuola* (see page 13) for both young boys and adult students. It consists simply of one large room with a blackboard and some chalk, a few books and many voluntary teachers. Yet in that air, too, there breathes the enthusiasm of Barbiana and a sense of the future.

A few words on the Italian school system might help the reader to understand the point of view and the criticisms of the young writers. Until 1962, when a law was passed making the three intermediate years' schooling compulsory, all children, starting at age six, were required to attend school for five elementary years only. They would complete the five years or repeat one or more. Yet, the earliest age for beginning work was not eleven but fourteen. Following the elementary stage was a school called *media*, intended for children who wanted to (or whose parents wanted them to) go on to the upper school (*liceo*) and possibly to a university.

The law of 1962 raised the working age to fifteen, established a new *media inferiore*, or 'intermediate school' (for twelve to fourteen year olds) and made it compulsory for all.

Today the Italian school system is organized basically as follows: five elementary and three intermediate years are compulsory. After fourteen, children who plan to continue their studies choose from a number of courses:

1. Five years of *liceo classico*, where Greek and Latin are taught as well as mathematics, sciences and so forth.
2. Five years of *liceo scientifico* (no Greek, some Latin and more emphasis on mathematics and science).
3. Five years of *istituto tecnico* (a technical school).
4. Four years of *liceo artistico*, where graphic arts are emphasized.

   (All of the above upper schools will qualify students for admission to a university.)
5. Four years of *magistrale,* a school that prepares elementary school teachers and qualifies students for admission to a *magistero* or teacher's college, which qualifies upper-school teachers.
6. Four years of a vocational school called *tecniche*.

It is very important to note that the school day runs only until 12.30 or 1.30 in the afternoon. Hence the great stress in this book on the potential use of the after-school hours (*doposcuola*) for those who need or want extra work. The well-to-do can afford to pay private tutors to complement the school work for their children. In poorer families those hours often go to waste, so that many children most in need of help are left stranded.

The marking system, a very rigid and rather dreaded feature of the Italian classroom, is the same throughout the elementary and upper school. It uses the numerals from 0 to 10, with 10 as the highest score, and 6 as the pass mark. General exams are given at the end of the fifth elementary year, after the third intermediate year, and at the end of the upper-school course. Make-up exams are also offered in September to the children who did not pass during the year and have prepared again for the tests during the summer.

Letter to a Teacher, written by poor country schoolchildren, has touched the lives of a vast number of readers. It has had great success in Italy, and in other countries. Undoubtedly, its popularity is in response to the book's substance, its attack on a very hot area of social and educational concern. The need for changes in the 'middle-class-orientated' schools of Italy is widespread and deeply felt, as witnessed by the turmoil among students in the past years. But the charm of the book in the original Italian comes also from its unique style. Italian readers, who are used to an overdose of adjectives, long sentences and ornate vocabulary, find this book direct, plain, refreshing. Its style follows what the boys call 'the humble and sound rules of the art of writing in all ages', which they set forth with typical brevity on page 25:

Have something important to say, something useful to everyone or at least to many. Know for whom you are writing. Gather all useful materials. Find a logical pattern with which to develop the theme. Eliminate every useless word. Eliminate every word not used in the spoken language. Never set time limits.

That is the way my schoolmaster and I are writing this letter. That is the way my pupils will write, I hope, when I am a teacher.

The 'I' of that passage is really a composite of the eight authors, all in their teens; the 'you' they address throughout the book stands for the kind of teacher they had all known in the school system. Their method of working as a team that can pool and trim its thoughts into such plain speaking is also set forth in a passage toward the end of the book (pages 103-4). Both the method and the result might well serve as models wherever a roomful of young writers would like to cut through accumulations of nonsense and tell some truths about their own world. The boys' clear and biting language may recall certain of our own writers who have sharpened their English against injustices, in the Orwellian mode; but the words from Barbiana seem especially strong to us, arising from within the world of the poor rather than being about it.

The writers are from Tuscan peasant families, but the experience they speak of is not limited to their own hillsides. While certain specific passages – their consideration of celibacy, for example, or their discussion of the use of the Gospels – may have a strange ring for some British readers, the main force of the book will have great relevance for people in many parts of the world. And even the 'strange' elements spring out of feelings universally recognizable among the poor in their quest for schooling.

This book is written to be 'useful to everyone', as the boys say. If the names Cicero or Homer come up, the boys supply footnotes explaining who they are. The message is for all to understand, and nobody is to be left out because he hasn't heard of certain books.

To back up their protest in depth the young authors did a great deal of research into the Italian school system. Their analyses of the data they compiled, which refer specifically to Italian situations and problems, may be hard going for a British reader. We considered editing some of these passages (particularly from pages 37 to 54), and omitting the more difficult charts in Part 3, but then decided against it. These children wanted to make more than an emotional protest. Under the leadership of Don Milani, they insisted that their conclusions also be accurate, and were willing to go through a painstaking discipline. Although some readers may only glance at the statistical work, its presence makes their moving appeal for change still more forceful.

In translating, we had many arguments about usage, about the finding of English equivalents for the fresh and often abrupt expressions the boys use, and also about the points they make. About schools, learning, about Italy and this country, about the future. It seems to us that kind of book: it stirs those who read it, not always or necessarily to agree, but to care. Its challenge is so direct, humane and radical that indifference to it seems almost impossible.

Nora Rossi
Tom Cole

March 1969

Part 1
The Compulsory Schools Ought Not to Fail their Students

Dear Miss

You won't remember me or my name. You have failed so many of us.

On the other hand I have often had thoughts about you, and the other teachers, and about that institution which you call 'school' and about the boys that you fail.

You fail us right out into the fields and factories and there you forget us.

Timidity Two years ago, when I was in first *magistrale,** you used to make me feel shy.

As a matter of fact, shyness has been with me all my life. As a little boy I used to keep my eyes on the ground. I would creep along the walls in order not to be seen.

At first I thought it was some kind of sickness of mine or maybe of my family. My mother is the kind that gets timid in front of a telegram form. My father listens and notices, but is not a talker.

Later on I thought shyness was a disease of mountain people. The farmers on the flat lands seemed surer of themselves. To say nothing of the workers in town.

Now I have observed that the workers let 'daddy's boys' grab all the jobs with responsibility in the political machines, and all the seats in Parliament.

So they too are like us. And the shyness of the poor is an older mystery. I myself, in the midst of it, can't explain it. Perhaps it is neither a form of cowardice nor of heroism. It may just be lack of arrogance.

The Mountain People

The school for all During the five elementary years the State offered me a second-rate education. Five classes in one room. A fifth of the schooling that was due me.

* *magistrale*: a four-year upper school leading to a diploma for elementary-school teachers [Translators' note].

It is the same system used in America to create the differences between black and whites. Right from the start a poorer school for the poor.

Compulsory school   After the five elementary years I had the right to three more years of schooling. In fact, the Constitution says that I had the obligation to go. But there was not yet an intermediate school* in Vicchio. To go to Borgo was an undertaking. The few who had tried it had spent a pile of money and then were thrown out as failures like dogs.

In any case, the teacher had told my family that it was better not to waste money on me: 'Send him into the fields. He is not made for books.'

My father did not reply. He was thinking, 'If we lived in Barbiana, he *would* be made for books.'

Barbiana   In Barbiana all the boys were going to school. The priest's school. From early morning until dark, summer and winter. Nobody there was 'not made for school'.

But we were from a different parish and lived far away. My father was ready to give up. Then he heard of a boy from San Martino who was going to Barbiana. He took courage and went to find out.

The woods   When he came back I saw that he had bought me a torch for the dark evenings, a canteen for soup and boots for the snow.

The first day he took me there himself. It took us two hours because we were breaking our path with a sickle and a billhook. Later I learned to make it in little more than an hour.

I would pass by only two houses along the way. Windows broken, recently abandoned. At times I would start running because of a viper or because a crazy man, who lived alone at the Rock, would scream at me from the distance.

I was eleven years old. You would have been scared to death.

---

*The intermediate school (*media inferiore*) covers the ages twelve to fourteen. See the introduction [Translators' note].

You see, we each have our different kind of timidity. So, in that sense we are even.

But we're even only if both of us stay at home. Or if you have to come and give us the exams at our place. But you don't have to do that.

The tables   Barbiana, when I arrived, did not seem like a school. No teacher, no desk, no blackboard, no benches. Just big tables, around which we studied and also ate.

There was just one copy of each book. The boys would pile up around it. It was hard to notice that one of them was a bit older and was teaching.

The oldest of these teachers was sixteen. The youngest was twelve, and filled me with admiration. I made up my mind from the start that I, too, was going to teach.

The favourite   Life was hard up there too. Discipline and squabbles until you didn't feel like coming back.

But there a boy who had no background, who was slow or lazy, was made to feel like the favourite. He would be treated the way you teachers treat the best student in the class. It seemed as if the school was meant just for him. Until he could be made to understand, the others would not continue.

Break   There was no break. Not even Sunday was a holiday.

None of us was bothered by it because labour would have been worse. But any middle-class gentleman who happened to be around would start a fuss on this question.

Once a big professor held forth: 'You have never studied pedagogy, Father Milani. Doctor Polianski writes that sports for boys is a physiopsycho. . . .'[1]

He was talking without looking at us. A university professor of education doesn't have to look at schoolboys. He knows them by heart, the way we know our multiplication tables.

Finally he left, and Lucio, who has thirty-six cows in the barn at home, said, 'School will always be better than cow shit.'

1. pedagogy: the art of educating children.
Polianski: we never heard this name, but he must be a famous educator.
physiopsycho: the first half of a big word used by that professor, we cannot remember the ending.

The peasants of the world   That sentence can be engraved over the front doors of your schools. Millions of farm boys are ready to subscribe to it. You say that boys hate school and love play. You never asked us peasants. But there are one hundred thousand, nine hundred million of us.[2] Six boys out of every ten in the world feel the same as Lucio. About the other four we can't say.

All your culture is built this way. As if you were all the world.

Children as teachers   The next year I was a teacher; that is, three half-days a week. I taught geography, mathematics and French to the first intermediate year.

You don't need a degree to look through an atlas or explain fractions.

If I made some mistakes, that wasn't so bad. It was a relief for the boys. We would work them out together. The hours would go by quietly, without worry and without fear. You don't know how to run a class the way I do.

Politics or stinginess   Then, too, I was learning so many things while I taught. For instance, that others' problems are like mine. To come out of them together is good politics. To come out alone is stinginess.

I was not vaccinated against stinginess myself. During exams I felt like sending the little ones to hell and studying on my own. I was a boy like your boys, but up at Barbiana I couldn't admit it to myself or to others. I had to be generous even when I didn't feel it.

To you this may seem a small thing. But for your students you do even less. You don't ask anything of them. You just encourage them to push ahead on their own.

The Boys from Town

Warped   When the intermediate school was started in Vicchio, some boys from the town came to Barbiana. Just those who had failed, of course.

2. We have also included in this figure people who live under worse conditions than farmers: hunters, fishermen and shepherds (*Compendium of Social Statistics*, United Nations, New York, 1963).

The problem of shyness did not seem to exist for them. But they were warped in other ways.

For example, they felt that games and holidays were a right, and school a sacrifice. They had never heard that one goes to school to learn, and that to go is a privilege.

The teacher, for them, was on the other side of a barricade and was there to be cheated. They even tried to copy. It took them one hell of a time to believe that there was no mark book.

The rooster The same subterfuges when it came to sex. They believed they had to speak in whispers. When they saw a rooster on a hen they would nudge each other as if they had seen adultery in action.

In any case, sex was the only subject that would wake them up at first. We had an anatomy book[3] at school. They would lock themselves up to study it in a corner. Two pages became totally worn out.

Later they discovered other interesting pages. Later still, they noticed that even history is fun.

Some have never stopped discovering. Now they are interested in everything. They teach the younger children and have become like us.

Some others, however, you have succeeded in freezing all over again.

The girls None of the girls from town ever came to Barbiana. Perhaps because the road was so dangerous. Perhaps because of their parents' mentality. They believed that a woman can live her life with the brains of a hen. Males don't ask a woman to be intelligent.

This, too, is racialism. But on this matter we cannot blame you, the teachers. You put a higher value on your girl students than their parents do.[4]

3. anatomy book: a book used by medical students. Analyses the human body in detail.
4. For instance, in the year 1962–3, 65·2 per cent of the boys and 70·9 per cent of the girls graduated from the first intermediate; 72·9 per cent of the boys and 80·5 per cent of the girls graduated from the second intermediate class (*Annuario Statistico dell'Istruzione Italiana 1965* [Yearbook of Statistics on Italian Education 1965], page 81).

Sandro and Gianni Sandro was fifteen; five feet eight in height: a humiliated adult. His teachers had declared him an imbecile. They expected him to repeat the first intermediate year for the third time.

Gianni was fourteen. Inattentive, allergic to reading. His teachers had declared him a delinquent. They were not totally wrong, but that was no excuse for sweeping him out of their way.

Neither of them had any intention of trying yet again. They had reached the point of dropping out and getting jobs. They came over to us because we ignore your failing marks and put each person in the right year for his age.

Sandro was put in the third intermediate class and Gianni in the second. This was the first satisfaction they ever had in their unhappy school careers. Sandro will remember this forever. Gianni remembers once in a while.

'The Little Match Girl' Their second satisfaction was a change, at last, in their school syllabus.

You kept them at the search for perfection. A useless perfection, because a boy hears the same things repeated to the point of boredom, but meanwhile he is growing up. Things stay the same, but he is changing. So the subjects turn into childish matter in his hands.

For instance, in the first intermediate year you read to the students two or three times 'The Little Match Girl' and '*La neve fiocca, fiocca, fiocca*'.[5] But in the second and third intermediate years you read things written for grown ups.

Gianni could not be made to put the *h* on the verb 'to have'.* But he knew many things about the grown up world. About jobs and family relations and the life of his townspeople. Sometimes in the evening he would join his dad at the Communist Party meeting or at the town meeting.

5. A story by Hans Christian Andersen, a Danish writer of the nineteenth century. '*Le neve fiocca, fiocca, fiocca*' [The snow is falling in flakes]: a line in a poem by Giovanni Pascoli [Italian poet of the nineteenth century – Translators' note].

* The verb to have is *avere* in Italian. The present tense is conjugated *ho, hai, ha*, etc. The *h* is silent [Translators' note].

You, with your Greeks and your Romans, had made him hate history. But we, going through the Second World War, could hold him for hours without a break.

You wanted him to repeat the geography of Italy for another year. He could have left school without ever having heard of the rest of the world. You would have done him great harm. Even if he only wants to read the newspaper.

'You can't even speak properly'   Sandro became enthusiastic about everything in a short time. In the morning he devoted hours to the same course he would have studied in the third intermediate year. He would take notes on the things he didn't know and at night he would poke around in the books of the first and second intermediate years. This 'imbecile' took your exams at the June session and you had to let him pass.

With Gianni it was harder. He had come to us from your school illiterate and with a hatred of books.

We tried the impossible with him. We succeeded in having him love not every subject; but at least a few. All that we needed from you teachers was to pass him into the third intermediate year and to give him lots of praise. We could have taken upon ourselves to make him love the rest.

Instead, a teacher said to him during the oral exam, 'Why do you go to private school,* boy? You know that you can't even speak properly?'

'___' 6

We certainly do know that Gianni can't speak properly.

Let's all beat our breasts about that. But most of all, you teachers, who had thrown him out of school the year before.

Fine remedies you have.

Without distinction as to language   Besides, we should settle what correct language is. Languages are created by the poor, who then go on renewing them forever. The rich crystallize them

---

*The school of Barbiana, a parochial school, was not part of the State school system [Translators' note].

6. Here should be a word that came to our lips that day. But the [Italian] publisher refused to print it.

in order to put on the spot anybody who speaks in a different way. Or in order to make him fail exams.

You say that little Pierino, daddy's boy, can write well. But of course; he speaks as you do. He is part of the firm.

On the other hand, the language spoken and written by Gianni is the one used by his father. When Gianni was a baby he used to call the radio 'rara'. And his father would correct him: 'It's not called *rara*, it's called "*aradio*".'*

Now, it would be a good thing for Gianni also to learn to say 'radio', if at all possible. Your own language could become a convenience in time. But meanwhile, don't throw him out of school.

'All citizens are equal without distinction as to language,' says the Constitution, having Gianni in mind.[7]

Obedient puppet But you honour grammar more than constitutions. And Gianni never came back, not even to us.

Yet we can't get him off our mind. We follow him from a distance. We heard that he doesn't go to church any more, or to any political meetings. He sweeps up in a factory. During his free time he follows like a puppet whatever is 'in'. Saturday, dancing; Sunday, the sports field.

But you, his teacher, don't even remember his existence.

The hospital This was our first contact with you. Through the boys you don't want.

We, too, soon found out how much harder it is to run a school with them around. At times the temptation to get rid of them is strong. But if we lose them, school is no longer school. It is a hospital which tends to the healthy and rejects the sick. It becomes just a device to strengthen the existing differences to a point of no return.

And are you ready to take such a position? If not, get them back to school, insist, start from scratch all over again, even if you are called crazy.

Better to be called crazy than to be an instrument of racialism.

*aradio: a dialect expression meaning *le radio* [Translators' note].

7. In truth we should say that the Members of Parliament had in mind the Germans of the Southern Tyrol but, unwittingly, they thought of Gianni, too.

Exams

The rules of good writing   After three years of schooling at Barbiana I took, in June, my exams for the intermediate diploma as a private-school candidate. The composition topic was: 'The Railway Waggons Speak'.

At Barbiana I had learned that the rules of good writing are: Have something important to say, something useful to everyone or at least to many. Know for whom you are writing. Gather all useful materials. Find a logical pattern with which to develop the theme. Eliminate every useless word. Eliminate every word not used in the spoken language. Never set time limits.

That is the way my schoolmates and I are writing this letter. That is the way my pupils will write, I hope, when I am a teacher.

The knife in your hands   But, facing that composition topic, what use could I make of the humble and sound rules of the art of writing in all ages? If I wanted to be honest I should have left the page blank. Or else criticized the theme and whoever had thought it up.

But I was fourteen years old and I came from the mountains. To go to a teachers' school I needed the diploma. This piece of paper lay in the hands of five or six persons alien to my life and to everything I loved and knew. Careless people who held the handle of the knife completely in their own grasp.

I tried to write the way you want us to. I can easily believe I was not a success. No doubt there was a better flow to the papers of your own young men, already masters in the production of hot air and warmed-up platitudes.

The trap-complex   The French exam was a concentrate of irregularities.

Examinations should be abolished. But if you do give them, at least be fair. Difficulties should be chosen in proportion to their appearance in life. If you choose them too frequently, it means you have a trap-complex. As if you were at war with the boys.

What makes you do it? Is it for the good of the students?

Owls, pebbles and fans   No, not for their good. You gave an

A— in French to a boy who, in France, would not know how to ask the whereabouts of the toilet.

He could only have asked for owls, pebbles and fans,[8] either in the singular or the plural. All in all, he knew perhaps two hundred words picked carefully for being exceptions, not for being commonly used.

The result was that he hated French the way some people hate maths.

The end   Instead, I learned my languages from records. Without effort I learned first the most useful and common words. Just the way one's own language is learned.

In the summer I had been in Grenoble washing dishes in a restaurant – I had felt at home right away. At the youth hostels I was able to be in contact with boys from Europe and from Africa.[9]

Back home I decided to pick up languages one after another. Many languages, even if not so well, rather than one to perfection. So I could communicate with all kinds of people, meet new men and new problems, and laugh at the sacred borders of all fatherlands.

The means   During the three years of intermediate school we had taken two languages instead of just one : * French and English. We had acquired a vocabulary sufficient to carry on any argument.

We did not linger over every mistake in grammar. Grammar is there mainly for writing. One can get along without it for reading and speaking. Little by little one gets it by ear. Later on, it can be studied in depth.

This is the way it goes with our own language. The first gram-

8. owls, pebbles and fans : These three words are more difficult than others in French. The old-fashioned teachers require students to learn them by heart in their first days of school.

9. Grenoble : a city in France.

   youth hostels : hotels for young people.

* One foreign language – generally French or English – is taught through the three intermediate school years. Records are sometimes available to students [Translators' note].

mar lesson comes when we are eight years old. After we have been reading and writing for three years.

Gramophone records are recommended in your own new courses. But records are good in a full-time school, where languages are learned for relaxation during the time when the boys are tired of other work. Every day of the week for a couple of hours. Not three hours a week, as you do it.

Under your conditions it is just as well not to use records.

The castles of the Loire   At the oral examination we had a surprise. Your students seemed to be bottomless wells of French culture. For example, they spoke with great knowledge of the castles of the Loire.[10]

We found out later on that this was the only thing they had studied all year. They had also prepared some selections from a syllabus and could read and translate them.

If an inspector happened to pass by, they could put up a better show than we could. The inspector does not venture outside the syllabus. Although you know perfectly well, and so does he, that that kind of French is useless. And for whom are you doing it? You do it for the inspector. He does it for the school superintendent. And he does it for the Minister of Education.

That is the most upsetting aspect of your school: it lives as an end in itself.

Social climbers at twelve   But your students' own goal is also a mystery. Maybe it is nonexistent; maybe it is just shoddy.

Day in and day out they study for marks, for reports and diplomas. Meanwhile they lose interest in all the fine things they are studying. Languages, sciences, history – everything becomes purely pass marks.

Behind those sheets of paper there is only a desire for personal gain. The diploma means money. Nobody mentions this, but give the bag a good squeeze and that's what comes out.

To be a happy student in your schools you have to be a social climber at the age of twelve.

But few are climbers at twelve. It follows that most of your

10. the Loire: a river in France.

young people hate school. Your cheap invitation to them deserves no other reaction.

English In the classroom next door there was an English exam. More baffling than ever.

I believe that English is the most useful of all languages. But only if you know it. Not if you have just started to scratch the surface. Owls and pebbles? The students could not even say 'good night'. And they were discouraged about languages forever.

The first foreign language is an event in the life of a young person. It has to be a success, or else there will be trouble.

We have seen from experience that for an Italian this success is possible only with French. Every time a French-speaking guest visited us, some of the boys would discover the joy of understanding him. The same night we could see them go and pick up the records of a third language.

The most important tools were in their hands: motivation, belief in a capacity to break through, a mind already under way on linguistic problems.

Mathematics and sadism The geometry problem in the exam brought to mind a sculpture in one of the modern-art exhibitions: 'A solid is formed by a hemisphere superimposed on a cylinder whose surface is three-sevenths of that. . . .'

There is no instrument that can measure surfaces. Thus, it never happens in life that we know the surface without knowing the dimensions. Such a problem can only be conceived by a sick mind.

New labels In the reformed* intermediate school things like that will be seen no more. Problems will have to be based on 'concrete considerations'.

And so Carla was tested on a modern problem on her exam this year, based on boilers: 'A boiler has the shape of a hemisphere superimposed. . . .' Back to surfaces again.

Better an old-fashioned teacher than one who thinks he is modern because he has changed the labels.

* The intermediate school, after the law of 1962, introduced new courses with a more practical intent [Translators' note].

A class made up of imbeciles   Our teacher was old-fashioned. The funny thing was that none of his own pupils managed to solve that problem. But two out of four of our pupils did work it out. The result: twenty-six out of twenty-eight were failed.

He went around saying he was stuck with a class made up of imbeciles.

The parents' union   Who should have kept him in check?

The principal might have been able to do it, or the teachers' council. They did not.

The parents might have been able to do it. But as long as you have the handle of the knife completely in your grasp they will keep quiet. And so, either we have to wrest from your hands all the knives (marks, reports, exams) or we have to get the parents organized.

A wonderful union of fathers and mothers able to remind you that we are the people who pay you; and we pay you to serve us, not throw us out of school.

It may turn into a good thing for you. People who get no criticism do not age well. They lose touch with life and the progression of events. They turn into poor creatures like yourselves.

The newspaper   The history of this half-century was the one I knew best. Russian Revolution, Fascism, war, resistance, liberation of Africa and Asia. It is the history lived by my father and my grandfather.

I also knew well the history of my own time. That means the daily newspaper which we always read at Barbiana, aloud, from top to bottom.

While cramming for the exams we would steal a couple of hours every day to read the paper, overcoming our stinginess. Because nothing is found in the newspaper that could help us pass your exams. This proves again how little there is in your school useful for life.

That is why we must read the news. It is like shouting in your face that your filthy certificates have not turned us into beasts. We want the diploma for our parents. But politics and the news of each day – they are the sufferings of others and are worth more than your interests or our own.

The Constitution   One woman teacher ended her lessons before the First World War. She stopped exactly at the spot where school could tie us to life. In the whole year she never once read a newspaper to her class.

The Fascist posters must still be dangling before her eyes: 'Do not talk politics in here.'

Gianpietro's mother was talking to her one day: 'But you know, I feel that my child has improved so much since he started going to the *doposcuola*.* I see him reading at home in the evening.'

'Reading? Do you know what he reads? The CONSTI-TUTION! Last year he worried about girls, this year it's the Constitution.'

That poor woman was made to feel that it must be a dirty book. That night she wanted Gianpietro's father to give him a good beating.

Vincenzo Monti   That same teacher wanted to teach her class, at all costs, the strange fables of Homer. Fine, if at least she were teaching Homer. But no, it was Monti's translation.[11]

We did not read it at Barbiana. Just once, for a joke, we took the Greek text and counted all the words in one of the stanzas. One hundred and forty words as against one hundred in Homer! Of every three words, two are really Homer's, and one is conceived inside Monti's pretty little head.

Who is this Monti? Someone who has something to tell us? Someone who speaks the language we want to learn? No, even worse: someone who wrote in a language not even used in his own time.

One day I was teaching geography to a boy who had just failed in one of your intermediate schools. He did not know a thing, but Gibraltar he called the 'Pillars of Hercules'.[12]

* *doposcuola*: 'after-hours school'; see the introduction [Translators' note].

11. Homer: ancient Greek poet, author of *The Iliad* and *The Odyssey*. Vincenzo Monti: poet of the nineteenth century. He translated *The Iliad* into Italian.

12. Pillars of Hercules: the ancient poets used to give this name to Gibraltar. It is the channel between the Mediterranean Sea and the Atlantic Ocean.

Can you imagine him in Spain asking for a ticket at the station window?

Order of priorities   If schooling has to be so brief, then it should be planned according to the most urgent needs.

Little Pierino, the doctor's son, has plenty of time to read fables. Not Gianni. He dropped out of your hands at fifteen. He is in a factory. He does not need to know whether it was Jupiter who gave birth to Minerva or vice versa.[13]

His Italian literature course would have done better to include the contract of the metalworkers' union. Did you ever read it, Miss? Aren't you ashamed? It means the life of half a million families.

You keep telling yourselves how well educated you are. But you have all read the same books. Nobody ever asks you anything different.

Unhappy children   At the gymnastics exam the teacher threw us a ball and said, 'Play basketball.' We didn't know how. The teacher looked us over with contempt: 'My poor children.'

He, too, is one of you. The ability to handle a conventional ritual seemed so vital to him. He told the principal that we had not been given any 'physical education' and we should take the exams again in the autumn.

Any one of us could climb an oak tree. Once up there we could let go with our hands and chop off a two-hundred pound branch with a hatchet. Then we could drag it through the snow to our mother's doorstep.

I heard of a gentleman in Florence who rides upstairs in his house in a lift. But then he has bought himself an expensive gadget and pretends to row in it. You would give him an A in physical education.

Latin in Mugello   In Barbiana we learned very little Latin. Parliament had buried it (with the new law).[14] In fact, that same

13. Jupiter and Minerva: the ancient Greeks believed, or pretended to believe in gods. They even used to say that a male (by the name of Jupiter) had given birth to a girl (by the name of Minerva).

14. The law originating the new intermediate school was promulgated in December 1962.

year Latin was no longer required for entrance to Cambridge and Oxford.[15]

But the farmers of Mugello still had to study it seriously. Solemn teachers moved among the desks looking like high priests. True custodians of the extinguished lamp.

I stared wide-eyed at this strange breed of men. I had never seen anything like them in my life.

The New Intermediate School

In your hands   We have been reading the new law and the courses planned for the new intermediate school.

Most of what we read we liked. Especially the fact that the new intermediate school does exist, is universal, compulsory and is disliked by the right-wing factions. These are positive facts.

But it is a pity to know that it is back in your hands. Are you going to make it class-orientated again, as it was before?

School timetable   The old intermediate school sharpened class distinctions chiefly through its timetable and its terms (short hours of schooling and long holidays). This has not changed in the new system. It remains a school cut to measure for the rich. For people who can get their culture at home and are going to school just in order to collect diplomas.

There is a sign of hope in Article 3 of the new law. It calls for the establishment of a *doposcuola* allowing at least ten hours a week. Just below that, the same article offers you a loophole for getting out of it: the *doposcuola* will be put into effect only 'upon ascertainment of the local conditions'. And so the decision goes back into your hands.

Results   During the first year of life of the new intermediate school the *doposcuola* was established in fifteen towns out of the fifty-one in the Province of Florence.

During the second year it worked in six towns, reaching 7.1 per

15. Cambridge and Oxford: old English universities reserved for gentlemen. No one could enter them, until recently, unless he knew Latin.

cent of the students. Last year only in five towns, for 2·9 per cent of the boys.[16]

Today no *doposcuola* exists in the State-school system at all.[17]

You can't blame the parents. They realized you aren't eager to get it started. Otherwise, willing as they are, they would have sent the children not only to *doposcuola* but even to bed with you.

Opposed   The mayor of Vicchio, before opening a *doposcuola*, asked the opinion of the State-school teachers. Fifteen letters arrived. Thirteen against and two in favour. The recurring argument was that if a *doposcuola* is not run very well, it is better not to have one.

The town boys were hanging around in the bars and in the streets. The country boys were back out in the fields. This being the case, the *doposcuola* could never go very wrong. Anything would be better. Even an abortive school like yours is better.

If you are opposed to the *doposcuola* let me advise you not to let it be known. People are malicious. They might think that you would rather tutor young gentlemen and earn a little extra on your afternoons.

South Africa   Some people hate equality.

A school principal in Florence told a mother: 'Don't you worry, madam, send your son to us. Our school is one of the least egalitarian in all of Italy.'

It is quite easy to cheat the 'sovereign people'. One can do it just by starting a special class for the 'nice' boys. It is not necessary to know them personally. It's enough to look at their report cards, their age, their address (farm or city), place of birth (North or South), father's profession, and influential references or strings.

In this way, two, three and even four intermediates will coexist in the same school. Class A is the 'intermediate old-style'.

16. *The New Intermediate School at the End of the First Three Years*, Ufficio Studi della Provincia di Firenze [Centre for Studies of the Province of Florence], June 1966.

17. '. . . after the brave experiment of the past few years which cannot be repeated on account of the negative attitude of the tutors in charge, no *doposcuola* programme exists now in the State-school system' (ibid., page 5).

The class that runs smoothly. The best teachers will fight to have it.

A certain kind of parent will go to a lot of trouble to have a child placed in it. Class B will not be quite as good, and so on down the line.

The duty to push But these are all honourable people. The principal and the teachers are not doing it for their own good, they are doing it for the good of Culture.

Not even the parents act for their own good. They are acting for the child's future. To push one's own way through is not proper, but to do it for the child's good is a Sacred Duty. They would feel ashamed not to.

Disarmed The poorest among the parents don't do a thing. They don't even suspect what is going on. Instead, they feel quite moved. In their time, up in the country, they left school at nine.

If things are not going so well, it must be that their child is not cut out for studying. 'Even the teacher said so. A real gentleman. He asked me to sit down. He showed me the record book. And a test all covered with red marks. I suppose we just weren't blessed with an intelligent boy. He will go to work in the fields, like us.'

Statistics

At the national level Here you might object that we happened to take our examinations in particularly bad schools. Also, that whatever reports we receive from elsewhere all happen to be sad. You can say that you know a lot of other examples, as true as ours, but leading to the opposite conclusions.

So, let us drop, all of us, a position that has become too emotional and let us stand on scientific ground.

Let us start all over, this time with numbers.

Unfit for studying Giancarlo took on himself a job of compiling statistics. He is fifteen years old. He is another of those country boys pronounced by you to be unfit for studying.

With us he runs smoothly. He has been engulfed in these figures for four months now. Even maths has stopped being dry for him.

The educational miracle we have performed on him comes out of a very clear prescription.

We offered him the chance to study for a noble aim: to feel himself a brother to 1,031,000 who were failed,[18] as he was, and to taste the joys of revenge for himself and for all of them.

The cocksure teacher   Scores of statistical compendia, scores of visits to schools or inquiries by letter, and trips to the Ministry of Education and to ISTAT[19] to gather further data, and whole days spent at the calculating machine.

Others may have done similar research before us. They must be the kind of people who can't translate their findings into plain language.

We haven't read their findings. Neither have you teachers.

And so none of you has a clear idea of what really goes on inside the schools.

We mentioned this to a teacher visiting our place. He was mortally offended: 'I have been teaching for thirteen years. I have met thousands of children and parents. You see things from the outside. You don't have a deep knowledge of the problems in a school.'

Then it is *he* who has a deep knowledge – *he*, who has only known pre-selected boys. The more of them he knows, the more he goes off the track.

Gianni means millions   Schools have a single problem. The children they lose. The Giannis.

Your 'compulsory school' loses 462,000 children per year.[20] This being the case, the only incompetents in the matter of school are you who lose so many and don't go back to find them. Not we: we find them in the fields and factories and we know them at close range.

18. Failed from the compulsory school during the school year 1963–4 (see sources in the Notes for Table A, page 116).

19. ISTAT: Istituto Centrale di Statistiche [Central Institute of Statistics].

20. This figure is taken from Table A (pages 118–19) and from the procedure in Table C, pages 124–6.

Gianni's mother, who doesn't know how to read, can see what the problems of the school are. And so will anybody who knows the pain endured by a child when he fails, and who has enough patience to look through statistics.

Then these figures will begin to scream in your face. They say that the Giannis run into millions and that you are either stupid or evil.*

The pyramid Since the statistical tables may be hard to digest, we have put them into appendixes. Here in the text we cut them down to a human measure. To fit into a classroom that can be embraced with one loving glance.[21]

We have decided to keep the pyramid diagram here.[22] It is a symbol that leaves an impression on the eye.

It looks as if it is chopped out by hatchet blows. Every blow, from the elementary years up, is a creature going off to work before being equal.

Tracing the class of 1951 But the pyramid does have the defect of putting students from age six to age thirty on the same sheet of paper – failures old and new.

Let's try to follow one class of children throughout their eight years of compulsory schooling.

---

*Here, from pages 37 to 54, follows a statistical analysis of the failure and dropout patterns in the Italian schools, demonstrating a powerful discrimination against the children of the working or farming classes. These are specifically Italian problems. However, the British reader may still be interested in these analyses and calculations as a sample of the way the students at Barbiana were taught always to make their point and base their findings on solid statistical foundations. Because of this serious effort on the part of these children, the Italian Physical Society gave a prize (generally given to promising physicists) to the school of Barbiana after the publication of this book [Translators' note].

21. We have imagined a first year of 1957–8 with thirty-two students. That is 29,900 times smaller than the actual number that year. Anyone preferring the actual figures can find them in Table C (for 1951) on pages 124–6.

22. All data used to draw the pyramid are taken from the *Annuario Statistico dell'Istruzione Italiana 1965* [Yearbook of Statistics on Italian Education 1965].

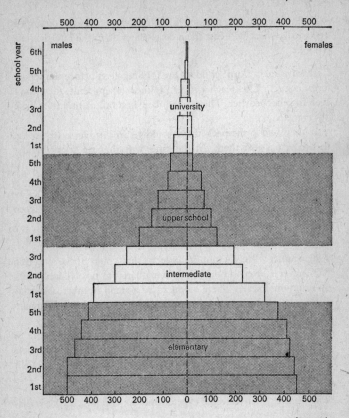

FIGURE 1 Children enrolled in the year 1963–4

Lacking more recent data, we shall follow the children born in 1951.[23]

First year Let us drop in on a first-year class on the first day of school, in October. Thirty-two students are there. At a glance they all seem alike. In reality there are five amongst them who will sit their exams again and again.

23. The children born in 1952 would have been preferable because they were the ones who inaugurated the new intermediate school. Too many data are missing, however, to make a thorough analysis of this class.

Seven years old, aprons and ribbons, yet already stamped 'retarded', which will cost them dearly later on in the intermediate school.

Lost earnings   Three children are missing even before the school term begins. The teacher doesn't know them, but they have been in school earlier. They tasted their first failure and they have not come back.

If they had come back they would be in her class. In a way, then, she has lost them. In the same way that we speak of lost earnings.

The same story goes on throughout the following years. To be really mean we could double the count of children lost every year: the ones you have chased away and the ones missing from your class because they are repeating a year.

To be really good, you should be the ones to do the counting.[24]

The truants   We do not include in our count those children who never started school. For them there are no available data on a national scale. There seems to be a small number, as far as we can tell. Giancarlo could not find a single one in the Mugello region.

We could not blame you for them, in any case. Others are to be blamed. Above all, the priests, who know the people of their parish and could have talked to the parents or even given their names to the school authorities.

The failures   In June the teacher fails six children.[25] She is dis-

---

For the moment we can only compare the two kinds of intermediate schools at the level of the first intermediate year. But this is sufficient to demonstrate that nothing has been changed substantially. When the children born in 1951 entered the first intermediate year of 1962–3 (old system) 33·3 per cent failed. In 1963–4 (new system) 28·2 per cent failed.

24. For more details, see Tables B and C in Part 3, and the Notes for these tables.

25. We noticed that in the first-year class of the previous year eight children were failed (three were lost and five repeated the year's work). The difference is due to the smaller number of children born in 1951 and repeating in 1957–8.

In the text, for simplification, we also refer to the children who withdrew during the year as 'failed'. In the Documentation in Part 3 the two groups are kept separate.

obeying the law of 24 December 1957, which asks teachers to bring them through the two years of the first cycle.[26]

But our young Miss does not accept orders from the sovereign people. She fails them and then leaves for the beach.

Shooting into a bush   To fail someone is like shooting into a bush. Perhaps you get a boy, perhaps a hare. We'll find out in time.

You don't know what you have done until the following October. Has he gone off to work or will he repeat the year? If he repeats, will he get anything out of it? Will he gain some solid ground for going on with his studies, or will he just grow older badly in courses not made for him?

Second year   In the following October the teacher* of the seven to eight year olds again finds thirty-two children in her classroom.[27] She sees twenty-six familiar faces and feels at home again among *her own*, whom she has come to love.

A bit later she spots the six new students. Five are repeating the year. One of these has already repeated it twice; he is almost nine years old.

The sixth new face is Pierino,[28] the doctor's son.

26. The elementary schools are divided into two cycles: first and second years (first cycle), and years three, four and five (second). 'Teachers will refuse to admit students to the next year in the same cycle only in exceptional cases (number of absences, psychophysical disabilities) and has to explain them in a written report to the Education Officer.' In the first five years of the new law 15·14 per cent were failed in the first year, 16·88 per cent in the second. In a good school (with differential classes, etc.) like the one in Vicchio, the failures go down to 6·9 per cent (1965–6).

* As a rule, a teacher stays with the same class for a certain number of years in the elementary schools. Throughout the discussion that follows, the elementary-school teacher referred to is one who has stayed with her class for all five years [Translators' note].

27. From here on, the reader might find it useful to keep in sight Figure 7 on page 52, or, even better, Table D on page 128.

28. In our text Pierino is the symbol of 30,000 children who skip the first year's schooling, each year. See Table E, pages 130–31.

Pierino The doctor's chromosomes [29] are powerful. Pierino could write when he was only five. He has no need for a first year. He enters the second at age six. And he can speak like a printed book.

He, too, is already branded, but with the mark of the chosen race.

Bitter bread Of the six failed children, four repeat the first year. They are not lost to the school but they are lost to their schoolmates.

Perhaps the teacher is not over concerned about them because she knows they are safely tucked away next door in another teacher's class. Perhaps she has already forgotten them.

For her, one boy – out of thirty-two – is just a fraction. But for the boy a teacher is much more. He had only *one* teacher, and she threw him out.

Two of the missing never came back to school. They are at work in the fields. In everything we eat now there is a bit of their illiterate sweat.

The mothers Six mothers have already learned what kind of a place your school is. Four have seen their children uprooted from their classes and from their friends. Exiled to grow up among younger and ever younger schoolmates.

Two of them have seen their children cut off for ever.

Mothers are no saints. They do not see beyond their own threshold. That is a great defect. But their children live on the same side of the threshold. They are people mothers can never forget.

Priests and whores Teachers, on the other hand, can always find excuses for forgetting. They are only part-time mothers. The missing child has the defect of not being there. At his old desk there ought to be a cross or a coffin, as a reminder.

Instead, a new student sits there. Another wretched little character like him. And the teacher is already growing fond of the new one.

29. chromosomes : those microscopic particles that control the likeness of children to their parents.

Teachers are like priests and whores. They have to fall in love in a hurry with anybody who comes their way. Afterwards there is no time to cry. The world is an immense family. There are so many others to serve.

It is a fine thing to be able to see beyond one's own threshold. But we have to be sure that we ourselves haven't chased a child away from it.

Only a fraction of equality At the end of the five elementary years, eleven children have already disappeared from the school, and it is their teachers' fault.

'Schools are open to all. All citizens have a right to eight years of school. All citizens are equal.' But what about those eleven?

Two of them are equal to nothing at all. To sign their name they make a cross. One of them has one-eighth equality. He can sign his name. The others have two-, three-, four-, or five-eighths of equality. They read after a fashion but cannot understand a newspaper.

Family allowances Not one of them is the son of well-to-do parents. The thing is so clear-cut that we can only smile.

Only recently have farm families begun to receive subsidies.[30] Fifty-four lire per day for each child. Workers receive 187 lire per day.[31] *

It isn't the teacher who writes the laws. But she knows they are there. Every time she fails the poor she leads them into temptation to leave. Not so for the rich.

Peasants This temptation to leave and go to work weighs on the children of both poor farmers and poor labourers. It can hit them at different ages. Those eleven boys who went to work during the five elementary years ranged in age from seven to fourteen.

30. 1 January 1967.

31. The allowances are actually a bit larger. But they are given for working days only, and the children of the poor have the vice of eating also on Sundays.

* Fifty-four lire is less than 9d.; 187 lire is about 2s. 6d. [Translators' note].

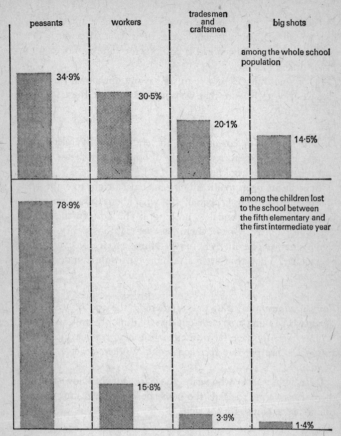

peasants | workers | tradesmen and craftsmen | big shots

among the whole school population

34·9%

30·5%

20·1%

14·5%

among the children lost to the school between the fifth elementary and the first intermediate year

78·9%

15·8%

3·9%

1·4%

FIGURE 2 Father's occupation

They were mostly peasants or, in any case, children living in isolated communities where even the smallest can be given something to do.[32]

Men before their time   The government has erased its memory

32. This should not need proof. However, in Figure 2, we have done a survey of a township in the province of Florence (school years 1963–4, 1964–5, 1965–6). In the 'big shot' category we have placed employees, teachers, professional men, businessmen and managers.

of these children. They are no longer registered as students but are not yet registered as workers.

Still, they are working, and by putting the following two laws side by side, we can really see what's happening even if it isn't acknowledged.

The law of 20 January 1961, 'On the Protection of Child Labour', forbids working before the age of fifteen. It does not apply to farm labour. Of course. This lower class has no children. We are men before our time.

Yet article 205 of the unified text INAIL* provides farm labourers with accident compensation from the age of twelve. This proves that it's known that we work at that age.

Mystery   A glance at the pyramid (Figure 1) gives some credit to the elementary teacher, despite all the children that she loses. The pyramid begins to take shape only in the intermediate years.

The teacher of the first elementary year began with thirty-two students. In the fifth, she still has twenty-eight. She apparently lost only four.

Actually, she lost twenty.[33] How she can lose twenty boys out of thirty-two and still have twenty-eight in class is something of a mystery and deserves explanation.[34]

The lake   Try looking at a lake on any map. It seems to have such a lot of water, but in reality it has exactly the same amount as the stream that fed it. The flow of water has simply slowed down. It loses time while taking up much more space. Then at the outlet it begins to run again and we can see that it is the same stream it was before.

The elementary years are the lake. A boy who is regularly

* INAIL : Istituto Nazionale Assicurazioni Infortuni Lavoratori (State Agency for Workers' Insurance) [Translators' note].

33. This and other data were taken from statistics on a national scale. Thus, this figure is lower than the real one, since it does not take into consideration the internal migrations (South to North, mountains to plains, country to city).

34. Professor Dinao Pieraccioni, member of the Consiglio Superiore dell'Istruzione (Superior Advisory Committee on Education), commented to a reporter (2 February 1967) about '. . . the low level of education of elementary-school students, who, as everyone knows, cannot be failed'.

promoted takes up five desks. When he repeats years he occupies six, seven, eight ... Pierino, that darling child, takes up only four desks.

When you stop failing pupils, you will in the same stroke solve the problem of crowded classrooms.

Nomads To the teacher, the Giannis, the habitual repeaters, are simply rubbish she has dumped into the laps of her colleagues. But what you do to others gets done to you. From the teacher next door you get just about the same amount of rubbish.

In all, for the five-year period the teacher has had forty-eight children in her care and handed on twenty-three of them. The twenty-nine Giannis passed through her class without leaving a trace. Of the thirty-two boys she was originally entrusted with only nineteen are left.[35]

It is forbidden to grow old The damage done to the eighteen students stranded in the wrong classes becomes serious at the intermediate level. They have grown old. And that is forbidden.

As long as there were five years of compulsory schooling the situation was different. Six and five makes eleven. Before reaching the legal working age there was time for two or three years of repeating courses.

But today six plus eight * equals fourteen. And a working permit can be obtained at fifteen.[36]

No time for failing At first glance it would appear that there is still time for one failure. But we need a second glance at the month of birth of these first-year children. The oldest boy in the group was born in January. He is six years and nine months old.

When you have checked them all you realize that three-

35. 11 gone to work + 18 repeaters = 29 lost to the class; 29 lost to the class + 19 survivors from first year = 48 passing through her hands.

* Six is the age at which children start school; eight is the number of years of compulsory schooling today [Translators' note].

36. Even this has to be looked at more closely. Some can find work illegally at ages thirteen to fourteen. Sometimes even 'legally'. In the year under consideration we found 129,000 children ten to fourteen years old who were working with a special permit (*Rilevazione Nazionale delle Forze di Lavoro* [National Census of the Labour Force], 20 October 1962, ISTAT, 1963).

quarters of the children are really older than six when they enter the first year.[37] So they do not have time to fail even once.

The Will to Fail   When a teacher becomes a victim of the Will to Fail she could let off steam on the children of the rich.

I would like to make a deal with the parents: 'Pierino is so young; he'll have to face so many choices before he is really mature. What do you say, Doctor, shall we keep him back for a year?'

The immature   But the teacher has a different opinion. Pierino is always promoted.[38] It's strange. Pierino, who is so young! The psychologists will tell you that he ought to be in trouble.[39] It must be the power of those chromosomes.

Pierino, at nine, finds himself in the class for ten to eleven year olds.[40] He has spent all his time among more mature schoolmates. He has not grown more mature but has been trained in the skill of facing adults. He knows how to be at his ease with you.

Gianni, instead, has always been in school with younger chil-

37. We simplified the data on the assumption that the number of births is the same every month and that the children apply for the first year as soon as they are of legal age to do so. Since we did not have a survey on a national level we tried to do it for two local communities and found the figures higher than three-quarters (79 per cent and 81 per cent).

38. *Exhibit 1*, offered in evidence: beginning with his starting school in the seven to eight year olds class, Pierino is promoted more easily than the other children. For example, in the year 1962–3, 87·6 per cent of the students as a whole were promoted, but 96·9 per cent of those prepared privately. This phenomenon of the advantage of privately prepared students continues through the elementary years. The opposite is true from the intermediate school on (*Annuario Statistico Italiano 1965* [Italian Statistical Yearbook 1965], tables 90 and 97).

Exhibit 2: the number of Pierinos does not diminish, but tends to increase as they jump subsequent years. In the second year (1959–60) there are 30,000 Pierinos. Four years later, in the first intermediate year, 34,000 (see Table E).

39. psychologists: people who think they can study the mind of a man in a scientific way.

40. Here, the ages are as of the first day of school. The division by age is taken from *Distribuzione per Età degli Alunni delle Scuole Elementari e Medie* [Distribution by Age of the Pupils in the Elementary and Intermediate Schools], ISTAT, 1963 (our Table E).

dren. He plays the bully sometimes, but when he faces an adult he is tongue-tied.

FIGURE 3

First intermediate year In the first intermediate year there are twenty-two children.[41] For the teacher they are all new faces. She knows nothing of the eleven who were lost. She is truly convinced that no one is missing.

At times she allows herself to grumble: 'Now that everybody comes to school it's impossible to teach. We get quite illiterate students.'

She has studied so much Latin, but she has never seen a statistical table.

The placard It wouldn't make a difference anyway. She would also have to study the ages of the students on her class list. Her students' childish faces and delicate bodies can be deceiving.

At the Registry of Births they don't bother to look at the faces. Whoever is old enough can have a work permit. He can run from your class at any moment.

Every one of these children ought to carry a big placard: 'I am 13. Do not fail me.'

Slaughter of the oldest But no one carries a placard. And the instructors look at the marks in their register books, not at the birth dates.

Some of them may act in good faith. Some may even want to save the older students. Then, facing a pupil's paper full of mistakes, they forget all their good intentions.

41. We keep the scale of 1 to 29,900 also for the intermediate school in order to have a clearer picture of the lost children. Actually, the number of classes in the intermediate years has decreased considerably; it decreases even further in the last years. This is why the teachers never see very small classes and do not realize how large a selection has been made.

The facts show that the oldest are always the ones who fail.[42] Those who have a job within easy reach.

But those children who are in step will go on being promoted. They had no reason to fail in previous years. They have none this year.

Not all of their houses are like Pierino's, obviously, but neither are they so very different.

The class gets mown down in this fashion: [43]

15   14   13   12   11

FIGURE 4

Slaughter of the poor   By failing the oldest of the children the teachers manage at the same time to hit the poorest.

We have made a survey of the professions of the fathers of those children who grow old in the elementary schools. The results can be seen in Figure 5.[44]

To bring home a pay packet   Gianni has already reached age fourteen and will have to repeat the first intermediate year. At this point, to continue becomes an absurdity. Even if he is passed each time from now on he will finish the intermediate school at seventeen.

42. See Table F on pages 133-4. As the statement we make is rather serious, we wanted to back it up with a particularly accurate investigation. Giancarlo has collected the data from Tuscan schools, and from two in Lombardy, one in the Marches, one in Emilia and one in Venezia, for a total of 1960 children in the first intermediate year and 1814 in the second (school years 1964-5, 1965-6).

43. In Figure 4 the students' ages are related for the end of the year, so the Pierinos are already eleven and so on. The sketch is based on Table E for distribution according to age, and on Table F for the age of the failures.

44. The data refer to the third, fourth and fifth elementary years in thirty-five schools of the provinces of Florence, Milan and Mantua for a total of 2252 students (school years 1965-6, 1966-7).

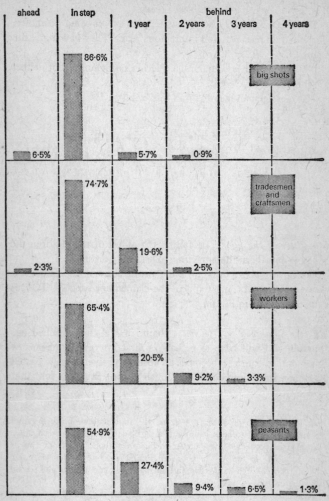

FIGURE 5 Slaughter of the poor

Boredom in school is at its peak. Work is easy to find.[45] In a few months it will even be legal.

Gianni is well aware that going to work is not all that great, but he does feel like bringing home a pay packet. He is fed up with being scolded for every penny he spends.

And his parents themselves make their protests with less and less force. To do otherwise, both they and the boy would have to have a very rare ability to persevere – a self-created passion for learning, strong enough to overcome every failure.

A helping hand from you could make the difference. You did stretch out a hand – but to topple him once and for all.

The vegetable man Perhaps that wasn't your intention. The teacher who stuck you with a student too old for your class is certainly guilty as well. The world may also be guilty and, for that matter, so may Gianni himself be guilty.

But when you see a little boy behind the counter of a vegetable stand, I would hate to be in your shoes knowing that I was the one who had failed him.

If only you were able to say, 'Why don't you come back to school? I've passed you, just so that you can come back. Without you, school somehow has lost its flavour.'

Second intermediate year By the second year of the intermediate school, the average age of the students is lower, since the oldest are missing. The distance between Pierino and the others grows less.

It can be said that the classes grow older all through the elementary years because of the boys who are repeating years. Then in the intermediate school they become younger again because the oldest have dropped out to go to work.

45. With the new provision regulating apprenticeship (law of January 1955) the engaging of apprentices has become convenient. In the more technically developed regions, children are sought out even in their homes, while their unskilled fathers may have trouble finding jobs. For instance, in the province of Florence, the city of Prato has a double pre-eminence: high industrial development and high truancy among school children. See *L'Adempimento dell' Obligo Scholastico*, Ufficio Studi della Provincia di Firenze [The Fulfilling of the Compulsory School System, Centre for Studies of the Province of Florence], 1966.

The role of the homes   The social structure of the school will change, too.

We have here a study made by friends of ours in a nearby township. They have subdivided the failures of the first and second intermediate years into social classes. The results are shown in Figure 6.[46]

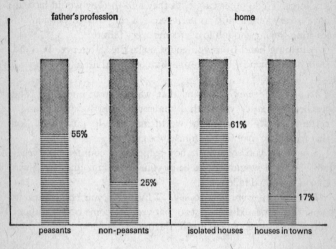

promoted

failed

FIGURE 6

When a test gets a 4   When the instructors saw this graph they called it an insult to their fairness as impartial judges.

The fiercest of them all protested that she had never sought out or received any information about the students' families: 'When a test is worth a 4, I will mark it with a 4.' She could not understand, poor soul, that this is exactly the charge against her. Nothing is more unjust than to share equally among unequals.

46. We call 'houses in towns' the houses in more densely populated localities and with all the facilities: water, electricity, roads and shops. The ones we call 'isolated' are generally on the slopes of Monte Morello or the Calvana.

Who is she talking about? Whether it's a matter of the age or
the social status of the students, the teacher starts breathing free-
ly when they reach the second intermediate year. She can cover
the rest of the course quite easily now.

She looks forward to June. Then she will get rid of her last
four thorns and will finally have a group worthy of her.

'When they came into the first intermediate class, they were
truly illiterate. But now, ah, their papers are all correct.'

Who is she talking about? Where are the boys she received in
the first form? The only ones left are those who could write
correctly to begin with; they could probably write just as well in
the third elementary year. The ones who learned to write at home.

The illiterate she had in the first year are just as illiterate now.
She has simply dumped them out of sight.

Compulsory And she knows it well. So well that in the third
intermediate year she fails only a few. Seven failures in first, four
in second and only one in the third.[47] Just the opposite of what
she ought to do.

In the compulsory school system, the compulsoriness ought to
carry all the students through to the third intermediate year.
Then at a final examination the teacher could release her selective
instincts.

We wouldn't say a word about that. If a boy has not learned
to write by then she would do well to fail him.

Summary Figure 7 on page 52 gives a summary of the class we
have been following throughout the eight compulsory years of
schooling.[48]

This class has lost forty children. Sixteen went to work before

47. For the same reason explained on page 46 we imagine the intermediate classes as very tiny. We are left with the impression that the
intermediate teachers fail fewer students than the teachers in elementary
school. In terms of percentage, it is quite different. Students failed: in
first elementary year, 15·4 per cent; in second, 18·1 per cent; in third,
12·9 per cent; in fourth, 14·9 per cent; in fifth, 17·9 per cent. In first
intermediate year, 33·3 per cent; in second, 23·2 per cent; in third, 5·1 per
cent. (See Table A on page 118.)

48. For the interpretation of this drawing, see Table D and Notes on
pages 127–8.

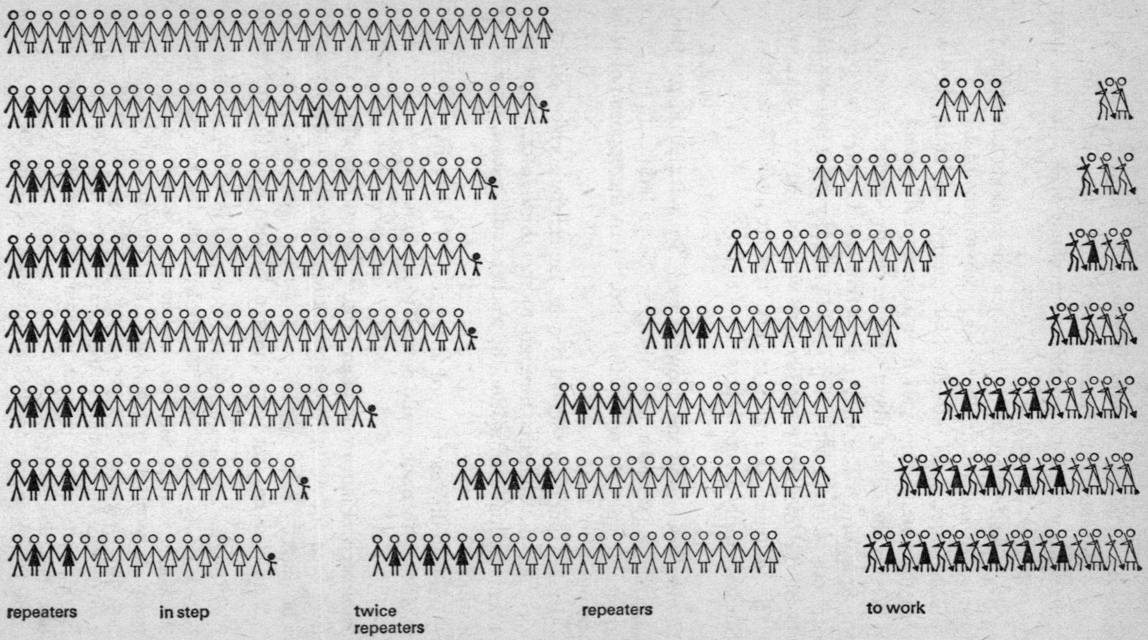

FIGURE 7

graduates from upper schools

children of businessmen and
professional men : 30 out of 30

managers and clerks : 7·6 out of 30

self-employed workers : 3·7 out of 30

dependent workers : 0·8 out of 30
dark figures = working children

FIGURE 8 Father's profession

they had completed their compulsory years of school. Twenty-four are repeaters. Altogether, fifty-six children have passed through this class. By the third year of the intermediate school we find only eleven out of the thirty-two original students entrusted to the teacher of the first elementary class.

Father's profession At this point we need a survey of the occupations of the fathers of the children who receive their intermediate diploma. The ISTAT has not made one. How could ISTAT think that a compulsory school system would make social distinctions?

But ISTAT has made a study of the occupations of the

fathers of students with upper-school diplomas. The result can be seen in Figure 8.[49]

These are the students who have had twelve or thirteen years of your kind of school. Eight of those years are compulsory.

It's not only money   Some of the children may have left school for lack of money, which is not your fault. But there are some workers who will support their children through ten or eleven years of schooling just to get them through the third intermediate year.[50]

They have spent every bit as much money as Pierino's daddy, but Pierino by the age of their children has already received his upper-school diploma.

Born Different?

The stupid and the lazy   You tell us that you fail only the stupid and the lazy.

Then you claim that God causes the stupid and the lazy to be born in the houses of the poor. But God would never spite the poor in this way. More likely, the spiteful one is you.

Defence of the race   It was a Fascist who defended the theory of 'differences by birth' at the Constituent Assembly: 'The Honourable Mastroianni, referring to the word "compulsory", points out that certain children have an organic incapacity to attend schools.' [51]

And a principal of an intermediate school has written: 'The Constitution cannot, unfortunately, guarantee to all children the

49. We settled on thirty children because the trouble of drawing a hundred children for each category was too great. The drawing assumes that all children of businessmen and professional men will finish upper school. The data are taken from *Annuario Statistico Italiano 1965* [Italian Statistical Yearbook 1965], tables 13 and 103.

50. Out of the sixteen children we saw in the third intermediate year, one received his diploma at age seventeen and two at age sixteen.

51. Constituent Assembly: Assembly of Parliament from 1946 to 1948. Beyond the usual parliamentary business, they prepared the text of the Constitution. The sentence quoted is taken from the discussion of Article 34 of the Constitution (compulsory school) at the First Subcommittee (meeting of 29 October 1946).

same mental development or the same scholastic aptitude.'[52]
But he will never admit it about his own child. Will he fail to
make him finish the intermediate school? Will he send him out
to dig in the fields? I have been told that in the China of Mao
such things are happening. But is it true?

Even the rich have difficult offspring. But they push them
ahead.

Others' children   Children born to others do appear stupid at
times. Never our own. When we live close to them we realize that
they are not stupid. Nor are they lazy. Or, at least, we feel that it
might be a question of time, that they may snap out of it, that
we must find a remedy.

Then, it is more honest to say that all children are born equal;
if, later, they are not equal, it is our fault and we have to find the
remedy.

Removing of obstacles   This is exactly what the Constitution
says, in reference to Gianni:

All citizens are equal before the law, without distinction as to race,
language, or personal and social conditions.

It is the duty of the Republic to remove the obstacles created by
economic or social conditions which, limiting the freedom and
equality of citizens, prevent the full development of the human personality and the full participation of all workers in the political,
economic and social organization of the country (Article 3).

It Was Up to You

Unloader of barrels   One of your colleagues (a sweet young
bride who managed to fail ten out of twenty-eight children in
her first intermediate class – both she and her husband Communists, and quite militant) used this argument with us: 'I did not
chase them away, I just failed them. If their parents don't see to
it that they return, that's their worry.'

Gianni's father   But Gianni's father went to work as a black-
smith at age twelve and did not even finish the fourth year level
of schooling.

52. Letter signed by a principal and eighteen teachers in response to the
critical study analysed on page 50 and in Figure 6.

When he was nineteen he joined the Partisans.* He did not quite grasp what he was doing. But he understood far better than any of you. He was looking forward to a world with more justice, where Gianni at least could be equal to all. Gianni, who was not even born.

This is the way Article 3 sounds in his ears: 'It is the duty of Mrs Spadolini [a teacher] to remove all obstacles. . . .'

And he pays you, too – quite well. He gets 300 lire per hour, and out of it he pays you 4,300.

He'd be willing to give you even more if you would work a respectable number of hours. He works 2,150 hours a year, while you work 522 (I don't count the examination hours; they are not teaching hours).[53]

Substitution But Gianni's father cannot by himself remove the obstacles that weigh him down. He has no idea how to discipline a boy going through the intermediate years: how long the boy should sit at his desk, or whether it is good for him to have some distractions. Is it true that studying causes headaches and that his eyes 'begin to trill', as Gianni says?

If Gianni's father knew how to manage everything by himself, he would not have to send Gianni to you for schooling. It is up to you to supply Gianni with both education and training. They are two faces of the same problem.

If you lead him forward, Gianni will be able to work with you in a different way and still be a more competent father tomorrow. But for today, Gianni's father is what he is. What he was allowed by the rich to be.

---

* Partisans: a guerrilla organization that sprang up throughout Italy during the Second World War to fight the Fascists and to help the Allied Forces [Translators' note].

53. The salary of an intermediate-school teacher, after taxes, ranges from a minimum of 1,223,000 lire a year to a maximum of 3,311,000 [from about £830 to £2,250 – Translators' note].
The number of teaching hours per year varies from a minimum of 468 (foreign languages and mathematics) to a maximum of 540. Minimum salary with maximum number of hours results in 2,264 lire per hour. Minimum number of hours with maximum salary: 7,074 lire per hour. In the text we quoted the mean, which is 4,300. Our data are updated to 1966.

Coaching   That poor man – if he knew what was going on he would pick up his weapon and be a Partisan again. There are teachers who coach for money in their free time. So, instead of removing the obstacles, they work to deepen the differences among students.

In the morning – during regular school hours – we pay them to give the same schooling to all. Later on in the day they get money from richer people to school their young gentlemen differently. Then, in June, at our expense, they preside at the trial and judge the differences.

The little civil servant   If some little civil servant did his paper work quickly and well at home, for a good price, but at his desk did the same job slowly and badly, you would have him locked up.

Consider further that should he whisper to clients, 'In this office your documents will be given to you late and all messed up. Let me suggest that you find someone who can do them better at home for a little extra' – he would be locked up.

But no one locks up that teacher whom I heard say to a mother : 'The boy's not going to make it on his own. Get him a tutor.' That's what he said, word for word. I have witnesses. I could bring him to court.

To court? To see a judge whose wife herself makes a bit extra by coaching? Anyway, the Italian Penal Code, for some reason, does not list such a crime.

Onions   You are all in perfect agreement. You want us crushed. Go ahead, do it, but at least don't pretend to be honest. Big deal, to be honest when the Code is written by you and cut to your measurements.

An old friend of mine stole forty onions from a vegetable garden. He got thirteen months in jail, no clemency. The judge of course does not steal onions. Too much trouble. He asks the maid to buy them for him. The cash to pay for both the onions and the maid is made by his wife, with her coaching.

Priests are more honest   Some parochial schools make a fairer showing. Although they play their part in the class struggle, at

least they don't try to hide it. At the school of the Barnabiti
Order in Florence, the tuition for a weekly boarder is 40,000 lire a
month. At the school of the Scalopi Order it is 36,000.*

Morning and night they serve the same master. They don't
try to serve two masters, as you do.

Freedom The other obstacle that you make no effort to remove is the sway of fashion.

One day Gianni told us, while talking about TV, 'They keep
feeding us this junk. If they led us to school instead, that's where
we would go.'

He used the impersonal 'they', meaning the society around
him, the world, that someone, not clearly defined in his mind,
who guides the choices of the poor.

We called him all sorts of names. 'But you've had two schools
already and you left both.' Just between us, though, did he really
have a free choice?

In town, all kinds of fads press down on him, never anything
worth while. When a boy doesn't follow the fads, he's 'out'. Or
he needs the kind of courage that Gianni doesn't have – so young,
so untaught and with nobody to help him. No help from his
father, who falls into the same pattern. None from the parish
priest, who sells games at the counter of the ACLI (Associa-
zione Cattolica dei Lavoratori Italiani).† None from the Communists, who offer games at the 'Casa del Popolo' [People's
Meeting House]. They all compete to drag him down deeper and
deeper and deeper.

As if our natural desires in themselves didn't give us enough
trouble.

Fashions A fashionable theory holds that the years from twelve
to twenty-one are for playing at sports and playing at sex, and for
hating studies.

The years from twelve to fifteen are the best ones for mastering
the language. And ages fifteen to twenty-one are the best for putting the language to use at union or political meetings. But these
facts have been concealed from Gianni.

*40,000 lire is about £27; 36,000 about £25 [Translators' note].
†Catholic Association of Italian Workers [Translators' note].

It has been hidden from him, too, that there is no time to lose. At fifteen it's good-bye to school. At twenty-one personal problems close in: engagement, marriage, children, making a living. He will have no time then for meetings, will be afraid to expose himself and won't be able to give fully of himself outside his home.

The defences of the poor   Only you teachers could have built a defence for the poor against the rule of fashion. The government pays you 800 thousand million lire a year to do so.[54]

But you are such paltry educators, offering 185 days of holiday against 180 * of school. And four hours at school against twelve hours out.† An idiot of a principal who walks into a class to announce, 'The education officer has granted a new holiday on the third of November', hears a shout of joy and allows himself a smug smile.

You have presented the school as a nuisance; how are the children supposed to love it?

Let's all embrace each other   In the town of Borgo the principal has granted the use of a classroom as a dance hall for the boys and girls of the third intermediate year. T' e Salesiani Order at their parochial school, not to be outdone, organize a masked parade. A teacher I know parades about with the *Sports Gazette* sticking out of his pocket.

These are men full of understanding for the 'needs' of the young. In any case, it's so easy to take the world as it comes. A teacher with the *Sports Gazette* sticking out of his pocket gets along very well with a labourer-father who also has the *Sports Gazette* in his pocket, while they talk about a son who carries a ball under his arm or a daughter who spends hours at the hairdresser.

Then the teacher puts a little mark in the mark book and the labourer's children have to go to work before they have learned to

54. *General Report on the Economic Situation in the Country*, 1965, vol. 2, page 495. The figure includes only the compulsory school.

* This figure excludes the thirty days of examinations, which the boys do not consider days of school [Translators' note].

† See page 61 [Translators' note].

read. But the teacher's children – they will go on with their studies to the last, even if they 'don't feel like it' or 'don't understand a thing'.

Selection Is Useful to Some

Fate or plan?   Here someone will start blaming it all on fate. To read history as keyed to fate is so restful.

To read it as keyed to politics is more disturbing: fashions then turn into a well-calculated scheme to assure that the Giannis are left out. The apolitical teacher becomes one of the 411,000 useful idiots armed by their boss with a mark book and report cards. Reserve troops charged with stopping 1,031,000 Giannis a year, just in case the sway of fashion is not sufficient to divert them.

One million, thirty-one thousand children *respinti* [rejected] each year. *Respinti* is a technical word used in your so-called school. But it is also a word used in military science. *Respinti* before reaching the age for conscription. It is not by chance that exams are a Prussian invention.[55]

Taxation   The curious thing is that the salaries that go towards throwing us out are paid by us, the rejected.

That man is poor who consumes all of his earnings. Rich is the man who consumes only a fraction. In Italy, for no clear reason, consumer goods are taxed to the last penny. But the income tax is a real joke.

I have been told that the economics textbooks call this system of taxation 'painless'. Painless means that the rich manage to have the poor pay the taxes without the poor noticing it.

At the universities such problems are often aired. But there are only gentlemen there. In the lower schools these discussions are forbidden. To speak of politics in school is not nice. The boss doesn't like it.

Who profits?   Let's try to see who profits from schools kept to a minimum number of hours.

55. See Treccani Encyclopedia under the entry 'Examination'.
Prussia: a region in Germany. It is commonly said that the military mania of the Germans comes from the Prussians.

Seven hundred and twenty hours per year means about two hours of school per day averaged out over the year. But a boy stays awake another fourteen hours. In well-to-do families these are fourteen hours of cultural improvement.

But to the peasants they are fourteen hours of loneliness and silence, good only for deepening their shyness. To the sons of workers they are fourteen hours at the school of the hidden persuaders.[56]

Summer holidays, in particular, seem virtually designed for the benefit of the rich.* Their children go abroad and learn even more than they do in winter. But by the first day of school the poor have forgotten even the little they knew in June. If they have to take any make-up exams they can't afford a tutor to prepare for them. Usually they give up and just don't take the exam.[57] Peasant boys help on the farm during the heavy summer months in order to pay for their keep.

Straight talk   At the time of Giolitti everything was spelled out: 'A convention of important men of property at Caltogirone suggested an amendment to abolish all primary education, so that peasants and miners will not absorb new ideas while learning to read.'[58]

Ferdinando Martini was just as frank. Lamenting that the intermediate schools had been made available to the lower classes, he said, 'It is for this reason that the members of the élite classes had to intensify their efforts or face losing all political and economic advantage.'[59]

56. hidden persuaders: advertising is called hidden persuasion when it convinces the poor that unnecessary things are necessary.

*The summer holidays last three to four months if the children are promoted in June [Translators' note].

57. We know many such cases, but it seeemed unnecessarily tedious to carry out a statistical survey.

58. *Memoire dalla Mia Vita* [Memories of My Life], Milan, 1922, vol. 1, page 90.

Giovanni Giolitti: Italian statesman; served several times in the government between 1892 and 1921.

59. Speech given at the Assembly on 13 December 1888.

Ferdinando Martini: Under-Secretary, then Minister of Education, from 1884 to 1893.

The Fascists   And during the Fascist régime the laws were quite explicit: 'Schools of urban or large rural centres will normally have a lower- and an upper-elementary school (five years). But those located in smaller rural areas will have, as a rule, only a lower school (three years).' [60]

Later, at the Constituent Assembly, it was again the Fascists who recommended lowering the school-leaving age to thirteen.[61]

Poor Pierino   But they were all alone. The other politicians have learned that one has to speak more subtly these days.

When the assembly was debating the new intermediate school, it was forbidden to speak against the poor. Nothing was left but to weep over 'poor Pierino' and the extinction of Latin.

A member of the Christian-Democratic party made the most moving speech: 'Why, indeed, should we punish the most gifted children, confining them in a school where *they* have to clip their wings, adjusting their flight to that of the slower children?' [62]

The Master

Does he exist?   We may seem to be implying the existence of some master who manipulates you. Someone who has cut the schools to measure.

Does he really exist? Is there a handful of men gathered around a table, holding all the strings in their hands: banks, business, political machines, the press, fashions?

We don't know. If we claim this, we feel our book takes on a certain mystery-story tone. If we don't, we seem to play the simpleton. It is like arguing that so many little gears have fallen into place by chance. Out sprang an armoured car able to make war all by itself, with no driver.

Pierino's home   Perhaps the life story of 'Pierino' can give us a key. So, let us try to take a loving look at his family.

The doctor and his wife are up there on top of things. They

60. Article 66 of the *Testo Unico* [Unified Text], 5 February 1928.
60. Article 66 of the *Testo Unico* [Unified Text], 5 February 1928.
61. The Tuminelli Amendment to Article 34 of the Constitution.
62. Honourable Limoni. Discussion at the assembly of the law setting up the new intermediate school. Session of 13 December 1962.

read, they travel, they see friends, they play with their child, they take time to keep close track of him and they even do it well. Their house is full of books and culture. At five I had mastered the shovel; Pierino, the pencil.

One evening, as if the decision has been brought about by the facts themselves, they say half-jokingly. 'Why place him in the first grade? Let's put him straight into the second.' They send him to take the tests without giving it another thought. If he fails, who cares?

But he does not fail. He gets all 9s. Serene joy fills the family, just as it would have mine.

Rain on wet soil   The one odd note in all this is that the young couple find a law cooked up just for them. The law forbids a five-year-old child to enter the first year class, but allows a six-year-old child to enter the second.

Is it a stupid law, or in fact altogether too shrewd?

Our young couple did not write the law. They hadn't even been aware of it before. But then, who did write it?

A special case   As it began, so it continues, year after year. Pierino is always promoted and he hardly does any studying.

I fight my way through with clenched teeth, and I fail. He also manages to have time for sports, meetings of the Azione Cattolica, or the Giovane Italia or the F. G. Comunista,[63] as well as time for his puberty crisis, his year of the blues and his year of rebellion.

He is less mature at eighteen than I was at twelve. But he keeps going ahead. He will graduate with full honours. He will become a graduate student at no pay.

Working gratis   Yes, gratis. Who would believe it; graduate students work without salary.

Here we come up against another strange law. It has glorious

63. Azione Cattolica : Catholic Action, the name of a Catholic political movement.

Giovane Italia : Young Italy; today it is a young Fascists' organization.

F. G. Comunista : Federation of Young Communists.

legal precedents. The Statute of Carlo Alberto[64] declared, 'The functions of an MP or deputy do not call for any compensation or emolument.'[65]

This is not a romantic disregard for material interests; it is a refined system for keeping out the inferior classes without saying it to their face.

Class struggle when carried on by gentlemen is gentlemanly. It offends neither the priests nor the intellectuals reading their *Espresso*.*

Pierino's mamma   Pierino, then, will become a professor. He will find a wife much like himself. They will produce another Pierino. More of a Pierino than ever.

Thirty thousand such stories every year.

If we consider Pierino's mother in herself, she is no wild beast. She is just a bit selfish. She has simply shut her eyes to the existence of other children, though she has not kept Pierino from meeting other Pierinos. She and her husband are surrounded by other intellectuals. Clearly, they don't want to change.

As to the thirty-one mothers of Pierino's schoolmates, either they don't have time or they don't know any better. They hold jobs which pay so little that to make ends meet they have to work from childhood to old age and from dawn to night.

But *she* was able to go to school until she was twenty-four. Besides, she was helped at home by one of those thirty-one other mothers – the mother of some Gianni who neglected her own son while doing the housework for Pierino's mother.

All the free time she gets to pursue her interests – is it a gift from the poor or is it a theft by the rich? Why doesn't she share it?

The lion's share   To conclude the subject of Pierino's mamma, she is neither a beast nor is she an innocent. If we add up thou-

64. Carlo Alberto: king of Piedmont, Liguria and Sardinia until 1848.
   Statute: a kind of Constitution on which are based the Italian laws from 1848 to 1948.
   65. Art. 50. It applies also to the functions of mayor and city councillor. Art. 50 was officially in force until 1948. In England, MPs have been paid since 1911.

   Espresso: a well-known weekly newspaper considered left of centre, and widely read by intellectuals [Translators' note].

sands of small selfish attitudes like hers, we get the total selfishness of a whole class, claiming for itself the lion's share.

It is a class that has not hesitated to unleash Fascism, racialism, war, unemployment. If it became necessary to 'change everything so that nothing would change',[66] it would not hesitate to embrace Communism.

No one can know the precise mechanism – but when every law seems cut to measure in order to serve Pierino and screw us, we have difficulty believing in chance.

Selection Has Reached Its Goal

At the university   'Daddy's boys' constitute 86·5 per cent of the university student body; labourers' sons, 13·5 per cent. Of those who get a degree, 91·9 per cent are young gentlemen and 8·1 per cent are from working-class families.[67]

If the poor would band together at the university, they could make a significant mark. But, no. Instead, they are received like brothers by the rich and soon are rewarded with all their defects.

The final outcome: 100 per cent daddy's boys.

In the political parties   The men who staff the various political parties, at every level, are solidly university graduates.

The proletarian parties are no different on this issue. Workers' parties don't turn up their noses at daddy's boys. And the daddy's boys, conversely, don't turn up their noses at proletarian parties. As long as they themselves get the prominent positions.

Indeed, it is quite *in* with the rich to work 'with the poor'. That is, not so much 'with the poor', as 'leading the poor'.[68]

66. The phrase in quotation marks is from the novel *The Leopard*. It is said by a Sicilian prince upon the arrival of the Garibaldi movement (1860). Later, he himself becomes a *garibaldino* and thus loses neither his money nor his power.

67. *Annuario Statistico Italiano 1963* [Italian Statistical Yearbook 1963], tables 113–14. All records on the following years are missing.

68. The height of political refinement today is to belong to a tiny party with no mass following (social-proletarian, or Chinese). A 'Chinese' demonstration in Florence during September 1966 was organized by students, all of whom were children of university eggheads.

The candidates   Politicians prepare the short-lists of candidates. They include the names of a few workers, as window dressing, in order to save face. But later on they see to it that university graduates get preference: 'Leave it to people who know their way around. A worker would feel lost wandering in the legislature. Anyway, Dr X is *one of us*.'

The legislature   To conclude, the men elected to make the new laws are the same ones who were quite pleased with the old laws. They are the only ones who have never personally lived through the things that ought to be changed, the only ones who should not be working in politics.

University graduates make up 77 per cent of Parliament. They are supposed to represent the voters. But voters with university degrees make up 1·8 per cent of the population. Workers and union members in Parliament – 8·4 per cent. Among the voters – 51·1 per cent. Peasants in Parliament – 0·1 per cent. Among the voters – 28·8 per cent.[69]

Black Power   Stokely Carmichael has been in jail twenty-seven times.[70] He declared at his last trial, 'There isn't a white man I can trust.'

When a young white who had given his entire life to the cause of the blacks cried, 'Not a single one, Stokely?' Carmichael turned to the public, stared at his friend and repeated, 'No, not a single one.'

If the young white man took offence at what Carmichael said, then Carmichael is right. If he is truly with the blacks the young white must swallow it, draw aside and keep on loving. Perhaps Carmichael was waiting for just this moment.

Newspapers of the left and the centre have always applauded any publication on the school of Barbiana. After this book, they may join with the right and start hating us. Then it will be clear that there is a party bigger than all other parties: the Party of Italian College Graduates, '*Partito Italiano Laureati*'.

69. 'Alphabetical List of Deputies', Rome, 1965, 1966. 'List of Senators', Rome, 1966.

70. Stokely Carmichael: Leader of the Black Power movement in the U.S. The Black Power people ask for power because they are tired of asking for equality and not getting it.

For Whose Sake Are You Teaching?

Good faith The good faith of teachers is a different matter entirely.

You teachers are paid by the government. You have the children right there in front of you. You have studied your history. You teach it. You should be able to see more clearly.

Of course, you see only selected children. And you got your culture from books. And the books were written by men in the Establishment. They are the only ones who can write. But you should have been able to read between the lines. How can you possibly say you are acting in good faith?

The Nazis I try to understand you. You look so civilized. Not a hint of the criminal in you. Perhaps, though, something of the Nazi criminal. That superhonest, loyal citizen who checked the number of soap boxes. He would take great care not to make mistakes in figures (four, less than four), but he does not question whether the soap is made from human fat.

Even more timid than I For whose sake are you doing it? What do you gain by making school hateful and by throwing the Giannis out into the streets?

I can show you that you are more timid than I ever was. Are you afraid of Pierino's parents? Or afraid of your colleagues in the upper schools? Or the education officer?

If you are so worried about your career there is a solution: cheat a little bit on your pupils' tests by correcting a few mistakes while you are walking up and down between the desks.

For the good name of the school Or perhaps you don't fear something so obvious and so simple. Perhaps you fear your own conscience instead. Then your conscience is built wrong.

'I would consider promotion of this child injurious to the good name of the school,' wrote a principal in his report. But *who* is the school? We are the school. To serve it is to serve us.

For the good of the child 'After all, it's for the child's own good. We must not forget that these pupils stand at the threshold of high school!' pompously cried the headmaster of a little country school.

It was immediately clear that only three of the thirty children in the class would go on to the upper years: Maria, the daughter of the dry-goods merchant; Anna, the teacher's daughter; and Pierino, of course. But even if more of the children went on, what difference would it make?

That headmaster has forgotten to change the record on his record player. He hasn't yet noticed the growth of the school population. A living reality of 680,000 children in the first year. Most of them poor. The rich, a minority.

It's not a question of a classless school, as he calls it. His is a one-class school, at the service of those who have the money to push ahead.

For Justice   'To pass a bad student is unfair to the good ones,' said a sweet little teaching soul.

Why not call Pierino aside to say to him, as Our Lord said in the parable about the vine trimmers:[71] 'I am passing you, because you have learned. You are twice blessed: you pass, and also you have learned. I am going to pass Gianni to encourage him, but he has the misfortune not to have learned.'

For Society   Another teacher is convinced that she has a responsibility towards Society. 'Today I pass him into the fourteen year olds class, and tomorrow he turns up as an M.D.!'

Equality   Career, culture, family, the good name of the school: you are using tiny sets of scales for grading your pupils. They really are petty. Too small to fill the life of a teacher.

Some among you have understood, but cannot find a way out. Always in fear of the sacred word. And yet, there is no choice. Nothing but politics can fill the life of a man of today.

In Africa, in Asia, in Latin America, in southern Italy, in the hills, in the fields, even in the cities, millions of children are waiting to be made equal. Shy, like me; stupid, like Sandro; lazy, like Gianni. The best of humanity.

71. Matthew xx.

The Reforms that We Propose

1. Do not fail students.
2. Give a full-time school to children who seem stupid.
3. Give a purpose to the lazy.

1 Do Not Fail

The turner   A turner at his lathe is not allowed to deliver only those pieces that happen to come out well. Otherwise he wouldn't make the effort to have them all turn out well.

But you, you can get rid of the pieces that you don't like whenever you wish to. So you are happy taking care of those who are bound to be successful for reasons that lie outside the school.

Lowest common denominator   This system is unlawful today.

The Constitution, in Article 34, has promised eight years of schooling to everybody. Eight years means eight different classes. Not four classes, each repeated twice. Otherwise Article 34 would be a poor word-play and unworthy of the Constituent Assembly.[72]

Today, to reach the last year of the intermediate school is not a luxury. It is a cultural minimum, everyone's right.

The man who doesn't get it is not an Equal.

Aptitudes   You can't hide any more behind the racialist theory of aptitude tests.

Every child has enough 'aptitude' to reach the third year of the intermediate school and to get by in all subjects.

It is so convenient to tell a boy, 'You are not cut out for this subject.' The boy will accept this; he is just as lazy as his teacher. But he knows that his teacher does not consider him an Equal.

72. In fact, the meaning was not questioned by anybody, neither during the meeting of the Commission nor during the discussion at the General Assembly. (See the transcript of the meeting on 29 April 1947.)

It is not good policy to tell another child, 'You are clearly cut out for this subject.' When he has too much fondness for just *one* subject, he should be forbidden to study it. Call his case 'specialized', or 'unbalanced'. There is so much time, later on, to lock oneself up in a specialized field.

By piecework   If all of you knew that, by any means possible, you had to move every child ahead in every subject, you would sharpen up your wits to find a way for all of them to function well.

I'd have you paid by piecework. So much for each child who learns one subject. Or, even better, a fine for each child who does not learn a subject.

Then your eyes would always be on Gianni. You would search out in his inattentive stare the intelligence that God has put in him, as in all children. You would fight for the child who needs you most, neglecting the gifted one, as they do in any family. You would wake up at night thinking about him and would try to invent new ways to teach him – ways that would fit his needs. You would go to fetch him from home if he did not show up for class.

You would never give yourself any peace, for the school that lets the Giannis drop out is not fit to be called a school.

You are the ones from the Middle Ages   On extreme provocation at our school we even use the rod.

Now don't play squeamish. Forget all those pedagogical theories. If you need a whip I can give you one, but throw away that pen lying on top of your record book. That pen leaves its mark all through the year. The mark of a whip disappears by the next day.

Because of that nice 'modern' pen of yours, Gianni will never in his life be able to read a book. He can't write a decent letter. That is cruel punishment, way out of proportion.

Mathematics   The maths teacher is the only one who might have some reason to complain if he can't ever fail a pupil. The second- or third-year lessons are useless to someone who has not learned the material in first year.

But mathematics is just one subject among many. The three hours a week of maths that a boy can't master should not cause him to lose all the twenty-three other hours in which he could do well.

Less is enough We could start a discussion here on the question of mathematics, similar to the one the Assembly had on Latin.

How much maths does anyone have to know for his immediate needs at home and at work? Or in order to read the newspaper? In other words, just how much mathematics will a non-specialized man of culture remember?

The ordinary maths taught in the eight-year course, except for numerical expressions[73] and algebra.

There is still the problem of making the word 'algebra' a meaningful part of the language. But that could be done in one lesson during the year.

2 Full-Time Teaching

Repetitions You are quite aware that two hours a week on each subject is not enough for every student to cover the whole course.

Up to now we have had a typical upper-class solution: the poor work through the year again. To the *petit bourgeois* you offer coaching (for money, after school hours) so that the lessons can be reviewed. For the upper-class boys it is all taken care of, since they are repeating what they already know. Pierino has had everything explained to him at home.

The *doposcuola* is a much better solution. A boy will repeat the work in the afternoon but will not lose the year, will not spend money, and will have you with him both in guilt and in struggle.[74]

Classless school Let's take off the mask. As long as your school remains class-orientated and chases away the poor, the only

73. numerical expressions: complex calculations performed during the intermediate years, unadaptable for solving any kind of practical problem.

74. We have avoided the problem of 'streaming'. Wherever it works out well it is the best solution you have. But if you run a full-time school you don't need it.

serious way to break the system is by creating a *doposcuola* that chases away the rich.

People who get upset at our solution but were never shocked at all the failing and private coaching are simply not being honest.

Pierino was not born racially different. He became different because of his environment at home, *after school hours*. The *doposcuola* must create a comparable environment for the rest of the children while keeping alive their own culture.

Environment   The words 'full time' frighten you. You feel it is difficult enough managing the children the few hours you do now. But the truth is that you have never tried.

So far you have run your class obsessed by the school bell, and with nightmares about the curriculum to be covered by June. You haven't been able to broaden the horizons, to answer the curiosity of your young people or to carry any argument to the very end.

The upshot is that you have done everything badly; you are always frustrated and so are the children. It is the frustration and not the hours of work that have tired you out.

One has to believe   Offer a *doposcuola* right through the elementary years *and* on Sunday, Christmas, Easter and throughout the summer holidays. How can anyone say that the children and their parents do not want something when it has never been offered to them?

A principal who merely sends faded copies of a circular to parents cannot say he has really tried to start a *doposcuola*. The *doposcuola* has to be launched like any good product on the market. Before it can be made to work, one has to believe in it.

Full-Time Work and the Family

Celibacy   A full-time school assumes a teacher's family obligations will not be a hindrance. A good example of a full-time school would be one run by a couple, husband and wife, in their home, open to everybody and with no fixed schedule.

Gandhi [75] did it. He mingled his own children among the

75. Gandhi: a saint of an Indian faith who lived in our century. He was killed in 1948.

others, at the price of seeing them grow up different from himself. Could you do it?

The other solution is celibacy.

Wife-machine occupation   Celibacy is not a word in fashion now.

The Church understood it, for the clergy, about a thousand years after the death of our Lord.

Gandhi understood it, for the sake of the school, when he was thirty-five years old (after twenty-two years of married life).[76]

Once, Mao pointed out for the admiration of his comrades a worker who had castrated himself (the Italian 'Chinese' are embarrassed to mention it).

88,000   You will need another thousand years before adopting celibacy. But, meanwhile, you can do something: start praising celibacy and use well the unmarried teachers that you do have.

Of the 411,000 teachers in the school system, 88,000 are not married. Fifty-three thousand out of the 88,000 will never marry.[77] Why not tell others and ourselves that this is not a misfortune but a blessing – to be available for full-time teaching?

It is common to say now, I don't know with how much foundation, that unmarried teachers are less human. The day celibacy becomes a selfless choice, teachers might grow passionately fond of the school, might love the children and be loved by them. Above all, they would have the joy of running a school that succeeds.

Full Time and Union Rights

Great fights   We happened to read a teachers'-union newspaper: 'No!' it said. 'No, to an increase in teaching hours!

76. His parents arranged his marriage when he was thirteen, according to the Indian custom at the time.

77. For this data we have based our calculations on the civic mortality records, with the assumption that teachers marry more or less in the same pattern as other citizens. As we can't foresee the future there is no other way to approximate the percentage of marriages of the living teachers. Separately: male single teachers, 33,000; females, 55,000. Fated to stay single: male, 14,000; female, 39,000.

There were great battles to restrict the compulsory teaching timetable, and it would be an absurdity to go back.' [78]

We felt taken aback. Strictly speaking, we can't say a word. Every worker fights to reduce his working hours, and so he should.

Unusual privileges   But your work timetable is really indecent.

A labourer works 2,150 hours a year. Your colleagues in the civil service work 1,630 hours. You, from a maximum of 738 hours (elementary teachers) to a minimum of 468 (maths and foreign-language teachers).

Your explanation that you have to study and to correct papers at home is not valid. Even judges have to write out their verdicts and sentences. Then, too, you could always skip giving tests. Or if you do give them, you could correct them, together with the children, while they are being taken.

As for your preparations and studies, we all have to study. Labourers need to study more than you do. When they take an evening course they don't ask to be paid.

To conclude, we repeat that your working hours are a peculiar privilege that the management has given to you for reasons of its own. It is no union victory.

Nervous breakdown   In the same newspaper we read further that your teaching hours are 'enough to drain the psychophysical capacities of any normal human being'.

A worker stays by his stamping machine eight hours a day, in constant fear of losing his arm. You would not dare say this sort of thing in his presence.

There are thousands of teachers, in any case, never too tired to coach paying students. Until you get rid of them, you are on the wrong side of the fence. It is hard to see you as workers entitled to union rights.

Strikes   For instance, the right to strike. It is a sacred right of every worker. But for a person with your kind of timetable to go on strike is disgusting.

78. *Il Rinnovamento della Scuola* [The Renewal of the School], 8 October 1966.

Study some more about Gandhi and you will discover other techniques equal in substance to the strike, but quite different in form.

A good solution for you would be to join the judges' union; you could go on strike just during those hours when your work is judges' work: exams, mark discussions, tests, reports.

If, instead, you stop working those few hours you are supposed to teach, then people will feel that you don't give a damn about us.

Who Will Teach Full Time?

School, with today's timetable, is a war against the poor. If the government can't impose longer hours of teaching, it should have nothing to do with schools.

This is a very serious conclusion. Up to now the State schools have been considered an improvement over the private. We might have to reconsider everything and put the school back in the hands of someone else. Someone with an idealistic urge to teach, and to teach to us.

Watch your words Let us keep our feet on the ground.

In the morning and during the winter, let the government run the schools. And continue to make them 'classless' (watch your words: the classism of the rich is called 'classlessness').

In the afternoon and during the summer someone else has to run them, and run them without class distinctions (watch your words again: a lack of class distinctions will be called 'classism' by the rich).

The town administrations A first solution is to confront the town administrations. Let them show whether their school politics is favourable to us. As for asphalt, new lights or playgrounds, even the Monarchists can provide them.

If the Provincial Administrative Board cuts down on the funds because 'it is not within the jurisdiction of the town government', the people of the town can argue that this law was made by the Fascists in 1931, and object to it on those grounds.

It is easy enough to put the blame on the prefect* and do nothing.

* The prefect is the head of the regional government [Translators' note].

The Communists It is possible that the town administrations won't budge. Even the Communists are timid when faced with class problems. Will they dare to antagonize the white-collar workers and the shopkeepers?

A big shot in the Party insisted that the schools must be the concern of the State 'when it is we who are in power. . . .' Twenty years have gone by since the liberation. The Communists have not reached that power. We're waiting for the grass to grow, but meanwhile the cows are dying.

The priests Perhaps the priests could run the *doposcuola*. But many among them cannot love with the same uncompromising love of our Lord. They believe that the best way to instruct the rich is to suffer them.

The union members The unions are the only working-class organizations. Therefore, it is up to them to get the *doposcuola* started.

The union members refuse to listen for the moment. They say that in a modern democracy each public institution has its own function and should not trespass on the others' grounds.

They, too, suffer from a certain timidity.

Still, they complain about the indifference of today's youth to everything. They say it becomes harder every day to organize people to strike, to sign up new members, to find activists and full-time officers. In the meantime they let the young grow up in schools run by the management.

At least give it a try After they have beaten their heads against enough walls, the union rank and file may change their minds. But meanwhile they could at least start some local experiments.

The CGIL and the CISL could try it, jointly or in competition.*

A school really costs very little: some chalk, a blackboard, a

* CGIL : Confederazione Generale Italiana Lavoratori (General Federation of Italian Workers) is a labour union.

CISL : Confederazione Italiana Sindacati Liberi (Italian Federation of Free Unions) is another large union [Translators' note].

few secondhand books, four older boys to do the teaching, and every so often a free lecturer to talk of newer things.

Full Time and Subject Matter

Don Borghi While we were writing this letter, Don Borghi* paid us a visit. He made this criticism of us: 'You seem so convinced that every boy must go to school and must have a full day of it. But then the boys will turn out to be apolitical individualists, like all the other students around. Good soil for Fascism.

'As long as the teachers and the subjects they teach stay the same, the less school boys have, the better off they are. A workshop makes a better school.

'In order to change teachers and subject matter, we must do more than write this letter of yours. These problems must be solved at the political level.'

Better than nothing That's true. A Parliament that reflected the needs of all the people, and not the middle class alone, could settle both you and the school syllabus with a couple of penal laws.

But first, *we* have to get into Parliament. Whites will never make the laws needed by the blacks.

To get into Parliament, we have to master the language. For the time being, then, and for lack of something better, children will have to go to your kind of school.

Professional deformity In any case, not all teachers are as bad as Don Borghi thinks.

It may be that your deformity began while teaching at those schools. You did not favour the little gentlemen out of malice; it's just that there they were, right in front of you, for so long. Too many of them, and far too long.

---

*Don Borghi: a priest, and a friend and collaborator of Don Milani. He was one of a small number of worker-priests who were at one time allowed to operate among the workers. When one of the translators asked the boys of Barbiana why they did not have an explanatory footnote on him, they answered, 'But everybody knows Don Borghi!' [Translators' note].

You became attached to them, finally, and to their families, their world, the newspaper they read at home.

Whoever is fond of the comfortable and fortunate stays out of politics. He does not want anything to change.

The pressure of the poor   But now things are changing. The school population keeps growing, in spite of you failing pupils.

With the masses of the poor exerting pressure, needing basic things, you cannot keep pushing a syllabus specially made for Pierino.

All the more so if you teach full time. The children of the poor will remake you and remake the syllabus.

To get to know the children of the poor and to love politics are one and the same thing. You cannot love human beings who were marked by unjust laws and not work for better laws.

3   A Goal

Religious schools   At one time there were religious schools that really were religious.[79] They had a goal and it was worth pursuing. But they did nothing for atheists.

Everyone looked forward to your great new secular solution. But you gave birth to a mouse: the school for personal profit.

The school with a religious goal is now extinct. The priests have asked to be integrated into the system, to give marks and diplomas like you. They, too, hold up to their children the God Money.

Communist schools   The Communists could propose a somewhat better school. And yet I myself would not care to be a teacher and have to trim my words. To see the doubts growing in the children's eyes: is he saying what is true or simply what is expedient?

Do we really have to pay this price for Equality?

An honest goal to be found   We are searching for a goal.

It must be an honest one. A great one. It must demand of a

79. religious schools: that is, schools which openly espouse and try to infuse in their students a given religious position.

boy that he be nothing less than a human being – *that* would be acceptable both to believers and atheists.

I know this goal. My teacher-priest has been impressing it on me since I was eleven years old, and I thank God for it. I have saved so much time. Minute by minute I knew why I was studying.

A final goal   The right goal is to give oneself to others.

In this century, how can you show your love if not through politics, the unions, the schools? We are the sovereign people. The time for begging is gone; we must make choices – against class distinctions, against hunger, illiteracy, racialism and colonial wars.

An immediate goal   This is the ultimate goal, which should be remembered from time to time. The immediate one, which must be remembered every minute, is to understand others and to make oneself understood.

The Italian language is not enough; it is not used very much around the world. Men need to love one another across national borders. For this we need to study many languages – living languages.

Language is made up of words from every subject matter. So we must touch all subjects, at least lightly, in order to enrich our vocabulary. We must become amateurs in everything and specialists only in the ability to speak.

Classic or scientific   When the new intermediate school was being debated in Parliament, we, the mutes, kept silent because we were not there. The peasants of Italy were left out when a school for them was being planned.

Eternal discussions went on between two factions, seemingly opposed to each other, but in fact the same.[80]

They were all graduates of the *liceo*, unable to see an inch beyond the school that had brought them to life. How could a young gentleman argue with his own shadow, spit on himself and on his own distorted culture while using the very words of that culture?

80. We don't say this in jest. Two of us have been patiently reading 156 pages of the records of the Assembly meeting.

Parliament split into two factions. The right wing pushed Latin in the school system. The left pushed science. None of them remembered us, not one had seen the problem from inside, not one knew the struggle that your school put us through.[81]

The men of the right were museum pieces. The Communists were laboratory mice. Both so distant from us, who cannot yet speak and who desperately need the language of today and not of yesterday – the language, not 'specializations'.

Sovereigns   It is the language alone that makes men equal. That man is an equal who can express himself and can understand the words of others. Rich or poor, it makes no difference. But he must speak.

The Honourable Deputy believed that we were all burning with desire to sew up somebody's intestines or to put 'Doctor' on our letterheads. 'The competent and deserving students, even the ones without personal names, have the right to follow their studies to the highest levels.'[82]

Let us try to educate our children to a higher ambition. To become sovereigns. Forget about 'Doctor' or 'Engineer'.

The social climbers   When we all have the power to speak, the social climbers can go on with their own studies. Let them go to the university, grab all the diplomas, make piles of money and fill all the specialists' jobs.

As long as they don't ask for a larger share of power, as they have up to now.

Wither away   Poor Pierino, I almost feel sorry for you. You have paid dearly for your privileges. You are marked forever by your specialization, by your books and by contact with people all just like you. Why don't you quit?

Leave the university, your obligations, your political parties. Start teaching right away. Start teaching the language and nothing else.

81. The Communist Deputy, De Grada, declared at the Assembly of 14 December 1962, that 'one learns to read and write in the elementary grades'.

82. Article 34 of the Constitution.

Break a path for the poor, forgetting about yourself. Stop reading. Wither away. It is the final mission of your class.

Saving the soul Don't try to save your old friends. If you go back to speak to them even once, you'll remain forever just what you have always been.

Don't worry about the sciences. There will always be enough self-seekers in that field. They will even make discoveries useful to us. They will irrigate deserts, fetch veal chops out of the sea, conquer diseases.

What do you care? Do not condemn your soul or your love for the sake of things which will keep moving forward anyhow on their own momentum.

Part 2

In the *Magistrale*
You also Fail, but . . .

England

The real test　When I passed my exams and left the intermediate school I went to England. I was fifteen. At first I worked with a farmer in Canterbury; later on, with a wine merchant in London.

In our school the experience of going abroad takes the place of your exams. But it is an exam and a school wrapped up in one. We test our culture by sifting it through life.

Our final exam is far more difficult than the one you give, but at least while taking it we don't lose time on dead things.

Suez　My exam went well. I came home alive and even brought back some cash. Best of all, I came back bursting with new experiences which I had understood and which I was able to retell.

The only member of the family who had ever gone abroad before was my Uncle Renato. He went to war, in Ethiopia. When I started to learn geography as a child, I asked him to tell me something about the Suez Canal. But he didn't know that he had passed through it.

Pacifist　You will never get me to go abroad like him, to start killing farmers. I went and lived in a farmer's house. There was a boy my age. A younger daughter, too. They have a barn, they grow potatoes, they toil away like us. Why should I kill them?

You are more alien to me than they are. But don't worry – I have been brought up as a pacifist.

Cockney　In London they are worse off than on the farms. We worked below ground in the City,[1] unloading trucks. My co-workers were English, but they could not write a letter in English. They often asked Dick to write for them. Dick sometimes would ask advice from me; I who had learned my English from records. He, too, speaks only cockney like the rest of them.

Fifteen feet above our heads were the people who spoke the 'Queen's English'.

1. the City: the London quarter where the important businesses are located.
cockney: the dialect of the poor in London.

Cockney is not very different, but to speak it is to be marked. The English don't fail students in their schools. They divert them towards schools of lower quality. In school, then, the poor perfect the art of speaking badly, while the rich keep polishing their language. They can tell from the way a man speaks whether he is rich and what kind of work his father does. Come the revolution, they can disembowel each other with ease.

Against a wall   When I returned to Italy I had forgotten that I was timid.

To explain oneself at the borders of countries, to argue with the boss and with monarchists, to defend oneself from racialists and queers, to save money, make decisions, eat strange food, wait for letters, and swallow nostalgia: I felt I had tried and conquered everything.

But one thing I had not lived through was the *magistrale*.* Now I've tried it. It has been like banging my head against a wall.

Either you or us   And yet, my schoolmates have broken through all over. Some of them are full-time union officials, and doing very well. Others are in various factories in Florence and nobody can intimidate them. They work in the unions, in politics and in the local administrations.

Even the two who went to the technical school have done well. They get promoted, like the Pierinos.

Our own culture bears up well wherever there is real life. In the *magistrale* it is useless.

Let's examine for a while what happened. It is either you or us. One of us is off the track.

Daily timetable   I had to get up at five to go to Florence. By motorbike to Vicchio, from there by train. It is hard to study in a train: sleepiness, the crowds, the noise.

I reached the front door of the school at eight and had to wait for the kids who had got up at seven. A four-hour handicap, every day.

---

*magistrale: the four-year upper school generally attended by prospective teachers. See the introduction [Translators' note].

Early timetable I was there on the first of October. But you
weren't. We were told to come back on the sixth. The students
of the 'Leonardo' School were told to report back on the thir-
teenth.

The responsibility for these delays is a mixture of saints and
sloth. Even Saint Francis is used as a pretext for stealing still
another day of school from the poor. After they have already
done without school for the four summer months.

Just where the responsibility for this laziness lies I haven't
yet worked out: within the schools themselves, or the school
governors or the Ministry of Education. They are all made up
of people who get paid on a thirteen-month basis.*

When a worker clocks in five minutes late he loses half an
hour's pay. If he does it often he can lose his job.

The railways are State-run, as you are, but they keep on going.
When we pass over a railway crossing we can be relaxed. The
signalmen are at their posts. Summer and winter, day and night.
If one of them fails even once, it will be spread over all the newspapers. He can't bring in excuses about work classifications, or
baby's tummy-ache. He goes to jail.

Why are you alone so special?

Perhaps the management finds it more urgent that trains
should function than that the schools should. They know that
their own children get taught right at home, but trains are a
different question.

The boss's only concern is that you be ready to give out the
diplomas in June.

Suicidal Selection

Forgetful In the first part of this letter we tried to show what
great damage is done to the discarded children. In Florence I
saw that Don Borghi† was quite right. The worst damage of all
is done to the select.

The child who gets promoted stays with the same class. He is
more of a fixture than his teachers. He should be able to make
friends with his schoolmates and to take an interest in how they
turn out.

* Most government employees receive an extra month's salary as a bonus
[Translators' note].   † See page 77.

But there are too many of them. Within eight years forty
schoolmates have been sliced away from him or have burned up
like dry branches. At the end of the intermediate school another
five have dropped out – even though they were promoted – and
so that makes forty-five. Pierino never hears a thing about them
or their problems.

Snooty In the second year Pierino was one boy among many.
By the fifth, he belongs to a more restricted group. Forty children out of the hundred he meets along the way have already become his 'inferiors'.

After leaving the intermediate school his 'inferiors' have mul-
tiplied to ninety out of a hundred. After the upper-school diploma they are ninety-six. After his college degree, ninety-nine.[2]

Every year he has seen higher marks put on his report card
than on those of his disappearing schoolmates. The teachers who
give those marks have engraved on his soul the impression that
the other ninety-nine belong to an inferior culture.

At this stage, it would be a miracle if his soul did not become crippled.

The poor have a reward His soul indeed is sick, because his
teachers have lied to him. The culture of those other ninety-nine
is not inferior; it is different.

True culture, which no man has yet possessed, would be made
up of two elements: belonging to the masses and mastery of the
language.

A school that is as selective as the kind we have described
destroys culture. It deprives the poor of the means of expressing
themselves. It deprives the rich of the knowledge of things as
they are.

Unlucky Gianni, who can't express himself. Lucky Gianni,
because he belongs to the whole world: brother to the whole of

2. 1961 census. See *Compendio Statistico Italiano* [Italian Statistical
Compendium], 1966, table 17. Children who left the elementary school
after passing their exams – 27,590,000 (60·5 per cent); those passing out of
the intermediate school – 4,375,000 (9·6 per cent); those passing out of the
upper school – 1,940,000 (4·2 per cent); those with a college degree –
603,000 (1·3 per cent).

Africa, Asia and Latin America. Expert in the needs of most of humanity.

Lucky Pierino, because he can speak. Unlucky, because he speaks too much. He, who has nothing important to say. He, who repeats only things read in books written by others just like him. He, who is locked up in a refined little circle – cut off from history and geography.

The selective school is a sin against God and against men. But God has defended his poor. You want them to be mute, and so God has made you blind.

Blind   Whoever does not believe us should go into town on the day of the *matricole* 'celebration'.[3]

The gentlemen feel no shame about their privileged position, and so they put on a hat to make themselves conspicuous. Then for a whole day they perform their antics in the streets, like puppies. They play obscene jokes, they break laws, they disturb traffic and everyone's work. They take off a policeman's hat and decorate his head with an enema tube.

The policeman takes it all silently. He understands his master's wish. But when the workers strike – serious, and orderly, moved by a desperate need – that is called disorder.

The young gentlemen busy with their tricks don't see that the policeman's servility is an accusation against them.

Nor do they notice the glance of a worker passing by without a smile. They are even capable of stopping him to ask for alms.

Kept men   Every worker gives alms every day, in taxes, even when he puts salt in his soup.[4] The students are studying at his expense. But either they don't know it or they don't want to know it.

A student in the intermediate school costs the poor 298,000 lire a year.* His father contributes 9,800 of that amount in school taxes. A university student costs the poor 368,000 lire per year. His father contributes 44,000 of that.

An M.D. has cost the poor, considering everything, 4,586,000

3. *matricole*: first-year university students.

4. The government tax on salt consumption brings in nineteen thousand million lire per year.

* 298,000 lire is approximately £200.

lire. The father has invested 244,000.[5] Later, with that M.D. degree which was a gift from the poor, the doctor will charge them 1,500 lire for a fifteen-minute visit, will go on strike against the *Mutua** and will oppose socialized medicine of the English type.

Potential Fascists Most of my schoolmates from Florence never read a newspaper. Those who do, read the paper of the Establishment. I asked one of them once if he knew who financed it. 'Nobody. It's independent.'

They don't care to know anything about politics. One of them did not even know the meaning of the word 'union'.

What they have heard about strikes is that they are a device for ruining production. They don't question the truth of this.

Three of them are out-and-out Fascists.

Twenty-eight apolitical plus three Fascists equals thirty-one Fascists.

Even blinder There are students and intellectuals of a somewhat different type: they read everything and are militant left-wingers. Nevertheless, they can seem even blinder.

The most left-wing teacher I have heard was giving a talk to a meeting of teachers and parents. When it came to the *doposcuola*, he burst out with: 'You don't seem to realize that I teach a good eighteen hours a week!'

The room was crowded with workers who get up at four in the morning to catch the 5.39 train, and with farmers who work eighteen hours every day, all summer.

Nobody spoke or smiled. Fifty blank pairs of eyes were fixed on him in silence.

The Goal

Bitter fruit The fruit of a selective system is a bitter fruit that will never ripen. I soon realized that most of my schoolmates

5. *Relazione Generale sulla Situazione Economica del Paese 1965* [General Report on the Economic Situation in the Country 1965], vol 2, page 495 (proof copy).

The university tax of 44,000 lire, which is among the highest, is for the medical faculty.

Mutua: the government's medical insurance [Translators' note].

were going to the *magistrale* either by chance or because their parents had made the choice.

When I appeared at the front door of your school I was carrying a new brief case. It was a present from my young pupils. At the age of fifteen I had already earned my first compensation as a teacher.

I never told this either to you or to my schoolmates. That may have been a mistake on my part, but your school is not a place for speaking out. When somebody knows what he wants, and wants to do something worthwhile, he is taken for an idiot.

Stingy   None of my schoolmates spoke of teaching. One of them said: 'I want to work in a bank. At the *tecniche** they give too much maths, at the *liceo*,* too much Latin, so I came here.'

The last census with data on the situation of these students is the one of 1961: 675,975 citizens have a diploma from the *magistrale*;[6] 60,000 are retired teachers; 201,000 were actively teaching that year; and 120,000 had applied to teach. There remain, then, about 300,000 citizens who could teach, but in fact do not (43 per cent).

Dissatisfied   Several of my schoolmates told me they would like to go on to the university, but without knowing in what field they wanted to specialize.

There were 22,266 graduates of the *magistrale* in 1963. The next year we find 13,370 of them applying to the university.

Thus, of every hundred who have the qualifications to teach, sixty are not planning to teach.[7]

Who can call himself a teacher?   One lone girl in my class seemed a cut above the others. She studied out of love of learn-

---

* See the explanation of the Italian school system in the Introduction [Translators' note].

6. In this census the figures do not include those who went on to take university degrees.

7. *Annuario Statistico dell'Istruzione Italiana 1965* [Yearbook of Statistics on Italian Education 1965], tables 152, 200.

ing. She read good books and closed herself up in her room to listen to Bach.[8]

This is the finest fruit that your kind of schooling can produce.

But I have been taught to find this fruit the most dangerous and tempting of all. Knowledge is only meant to be passed on. 'A man can call himself a teacher when he has no cultural interest just for his own sake.'

A closed school   I know it must be discouraging for you to try to explain what a teacher is to the kind of boys you have in your classes. Still – is it the boys who have ruined you, or is it you who have ruined them?

Because of the increasing possibility to apply to the university after the *magistrale* instead of going into teaching, the training in the *magistrale* is becoming ever more generalized and vague.

To produce good teachers we need a self-contained school, one that is not a stepping-stone to other fields. The boy who wants to work in a bank should feel like an outsider in such a school. The boy from the farms who has chosen to become a teacher should feel at home.

A necessary selection   Now we come up against a problem wholly different from that of the compulsory eight-year school. There, everyone has the sacred right to be made equal. In the *magistrale* it is strictly a question of qualifications.

These schools educate citizens specialized in serving others. They have to be reliable.

The teaching diploma should be hard to get. We don't want to be cut down later on. We should be treated the same as chemists, doctors and engineers.

An eye on the goal   You do not fail a taxi driver if he doesn't know maths, or a doctor who doesn't know his poets.

Once you said to me, in these precise words, 'You see, you don't know enough Latin. Why don't you go to a technical school?'

8. Bach: German musician of the eighteenth century.

Are you sure that Latin is indispensable to the making of a good teacher? Have you given it any thought? All you do is keep your eye on the system as it is; but you never really evaluate it.

The individual   If you had taken a real interest in me, enough to ask yourself where I came from, who I was, where I was heading, then your Latin would have gone out of focus.

But you might have found something else to object to in me. It frightens you to see a fifteen-year-old boy who knows what he wants. You sense the influence of his teacher.

Woe unto him who toys with the Individual! The Free Development of the Personality is your highest creed. The needs of society are no concern of yours at all.

I am a boy under the influence of my teacher and I am proud of it. He, too, is proud of it. What, if not this, is the essence of a school?

School is the one difference between men and animals. The teacher gives to a boy everything the teacher himself believes, loves and hopes for. The boy, growing up, will add something of his own, and this is the way humanity moves forward.

Animals don't go to school. In the Free Development of their Personality, swallows have built their nests in exactly the same way for millenniums.

The seminary   I have been told that even in the seminary there are boys torturing themselves to find *their* vocation. If they had been told in elementary school that we all have the same vocation – to do good wherever we are – then they would not have to lose the best years of their lives worrying about themselves.

School of Social Service   We could allow a bit more time for final choices by having two different types of schools.

One, for fourteen to eighteen year olds, could be called the 'School of Social Service'. It would be for anybody who has already decided to give his life to others. The same schooling could serve for priests, elementary school teachers, union workers and men in politics. One year might be added for specialization.

We could call all the other schools 'Schools of Ego Service', and they could continue to be the schools that we have now, without changing them.

High aims The School of Social Service could try to aim high and find pleasure in it. No marks, no mark book, no games, no holidays, no weakness about marriage or a career. All the students would be guided toward total dedication.

Along the way some might settle a bit lower. They might find girls and adjust themselves to loving a more limited family.

They will be much better off for having spent their best years preparing to serve an immense family – the family of man. They will make better fathers and mothers, full of ideals, ready to raise a child who in turn will go back to that same school.

Your School of Ego Service wants to prepare everyone for marriage. It is not much of a success even for those who marry. And when someone stays single, he becomes a bitter spinsterman.

Unemployed teachers We often hear complaints that there are too many teachers. That is not true. Teaching is the kind of profession that attracts many who really don't like it at all. Increase the hours of work and all of them will drop out.

A married female teacher makes as much money as her husband. Actually she spends no more time out of her home than a housewife. A perfect wife and mother. She stays home every time the child catches cold. Who wouldn't want a woman like that for a wife?

Then there are thousands of unfilled positions in the intermediate school. You fill them with anyone who has any higher degree at all or is studying for a degree (chemists, veterinary surgeons, pseudostudents).

You have refused to give those positions to elementary teachers with years of experience in the classroom.

Caste system The legislators now in power will never open the doors of the intermediate school to graduates of the *magistrale*.

On the contrary, some are proposing a university degree as a requirement for teaching even in the elementary schools. They say that pedagogy and psychology, as sciences, have to be studied at the university level.

When university graduates criticize the school and call it sick, they forget that they are products of it. They fed on this poison up to the age of twenty-five. They are unable to imagine that people with different backgrounds can also be worth something.

When they speak with the elementary teachers of their little children, they talk to them as to members of the family. They don't hide a thing; they work together.

But when they speak to a teacher in the intermediate school, they measure their words as if they were facing an enemy.

They don't want to admit it, but they do know the truth. The elementary teachers are good because they did not spend so much time in school. The teachers in the upper schools are what they are because they all have those degrees.

The Culture Needed by All

Exodus In the mountains we can't survive. In the fields there are too many of us. All the economists agree on that point.

And what if they didn't agree? Try and put yourself in my parents' shoes. You would not allow your son to be shunted aside. Therefore, you ought to welcome us in your midst – and not as a second-class citizens good only for unskilled work.

Every People has its own culture, and no People has less than the others. Our culture is a gift that we bring to you. A vital breath of air to relieve the dryness of your books written by men who have done nothing but read books.

Agrarian culture Glancing through the pages of a school text-book we see plants, animals, the seasons. It seems that only a peasant could have written it.

But no, the authors are products of your school. It's enough just to glance at the pictures: left-handed farmers, round shovels, hooked hoes, blacksmiths with tools used in Roman times, cherry trees with the leaves of plum trees.

My first-year teacher told me one day, 'Climb that tree and pick some cherries for me.' When my mother heard this, she said, 'Whoever gave her a teaching licence?'

You gave her a teaching licence but you deny me one, when I know all my trees, each by each.

I also know my *sormenti*.* I have pruned them, gathered them, used them to bake bread. In one of my papers you underlined '*sormenti*' as a mistake. You insisted that the word is '*sarmenti*' because it comes from Latin. Then you sneaked away to look up its meaning in the dictionary.

All alone, like dogs You know even less about men than we do. The lift serves as a good machine for ignoring the people in your building; the car, for ignoring people who travel in buses; the telephone, for avoiding seeing people's faces or entering their homes.

I don't know about you, but your students who know Cicero[9] – how many families of living men do they know intimately? How many of their kitchens have they visited? How many of their sick have they sat with through the night? How many of their dead have they borne on their shoulders? How many can they trust when they are in distress?

If it hadn't been for the flood in Florence,† they wouldn't know how many people there are in the family that lives on the ground floor.

I was in a class for a year with these young people, but I have no idea what their families are like. And yet they never stop jabbering. Often they raise their voices to a pitch so high no one can possibly understand them. In any case, each one only wants to listen to himself.

Human culture A thousand motors roar under your windows every day. You have no idea to whom they belong or where they are going.

But I can read the sounds of my valley for miles around. The sound of the motor in the distance is Nevio going to the station, a little late. If you like, I can tell you everything about hundreds of people, dozens of families and their relatives and personal ties.

Whenever you speak to a worker you manage to get it all wrong: your choice of words, your tone, your jokes. I can tell

* *sormenti* : twigs; vine-shoots [Translators' note].

9. Cicero : a Latin writer.

† The great flood of 1966 [Translators' note].

what a mountaineer is thinking even when he keeps silent, and I know what's on his mind even when he talks about something else.

This is the sort of culture your poets should have given you. It is the culture of nine-tenths of the earth, but no one has yet managed to put it down in words or pictures or films.

Be a bit humble, at least. Your culture has gaps as wide as ours. Perhaps even wider. Certainly more damaging to a teacher in the elementary schools.

The Culture that You Demand of Us

Latin Your most important subject is one we shall never have to teach.

You even have us translate from Italian into Latin. But who can draw the exact line where Latin ends and Italian begins?

Somebody or other even wrote a Latin grammar for you. It is a major swindle. Because for every rule, one should know when and where it really originates.

Conformists accept the imposition of grammar and learn all the rules by heart. The one thing they care about is promotion. In turn, they will play the same rule-book game when they themselves are teachers.

You underlined the word '*portavit*' [10] in one paper of mine. According to you it is a crime to try to simplify anything when it can be made complicated. The curious fact is that Cicero often used '*porto*'. 'He was a Roman and didn't even know it.' [11]

Mathematics The second subject badly taught in the *magistrale* is maths. To teach at the elementary level it is enough to know elementary maths. The mathematics of the three intermediate years is merely an extra. In fact, in the *magistrale* course all maths could be eliminated. Instead, one should learn the best way to teach maths – which in itself is not maths, but has to do with the learning process or with pedagogy.

10. *portavit* : two verbs in Latin mean to carry. One is easy (*porto*), the other difficult (*fero*).

11. A line from the poem 'The Discovery of America' by Pascarella (a poet who writes in Roman dialect).

Some higher mathematics, as an aspect of our general culture, could be taught in two or three lectures given by a specialist who can explain in a few words what it is all about.

The problem will not essentially change even if teachers graduating from the *magistrale* also have to teach the intermediate years in the future.

In truth, a mathematics degree is not necessary for teaching maths at the intermediate level. That need was invented by the special caste of people who have children with university degrees. This way they pocket 20,478 quite desirable jobs: minimum work load (sixteen hours per week), and no need to keep on your toes. In such a job you can repeat year after year the same idiocies that any student in the third intermediate class already knows. It is a job that requires only fifteen minutes for correcting all your students' papers, because the answers are either right or wrong.

Philosophy Any philosopher studied out of a handbook becomes a bore.[12] There are too many philosophers and they say too many things.

My philosophy teacher never took a stand for or against any of them. I could not work out whether he liked them all or simply didn't care.

If I have to choose between two teachers, one a nut on the subject and the other totally indifferent, I'll take the nut – the one who has a theory of his own, or prefers a particular philosopher. He is certain to talk only about that philosopher and to attack all the others, but he would make us read the original writings of that philosopher during all of our three years of school. We would come out knowing that philosophy can fill an entire life.

Pedagogy The way pedagogy is taught today, I would skip it altogether – although I'm not quite sure. Perhaps if we go deeper into it, we could decide whether or not it has something to say.

We might discover that it says one thing, and one thing only. That each boy is different, each historical moment is different,

12. philosopher: a thinker.
handbook: a book summarizing the writing of many philosophers.

and so is every moment different for each boy, each country, each environment, each family.

Half a page from the textbook is all that is needed to explain this; the rest we can tear up and throw away.

At the school of Barbiana not a day went by without its pedagogical problem. But we never called it by that name. For us, it always had the name of a particular boy. Case after case, time after time.

I don't think there is a treatise written by any professor that can tell us anything about Gianni that we don't already know.

The Gospels   Three years spent on bad translations of ancient poems (the *Iliad*, the *Odyssey*, the *Aeneid*). Three years reading Dante. And not a minute spent on the Gospels.

Don't make the claim that the Gospels are strictly the concern of the clergy. Leaving aside the religious issue, the book remains a book to be read in every school and in every year.

In courses on literature the longest period should be given to studying the book that has left the deepest trace, the one which has crossed all frontiers.

The longest chapter in geography class should be Palestine. In history, on the events that preceded, accompanied and followed the life of our Lord.

A special area of subject matter should be added to the syllabus: the reading of the Old Testament, a study of the synoptic Gospels, textual criticism, and related questions of linguistics and archaeology.[13]

Why didn't you think of it? Can it be that the men who planned your school hold Jesus in distrust: too good a friend of the poor, too poor a friend of possessions?

Religion   When the Gospels receive the place they deserve, then the teaching of religion will become a serious matter.

It will simply be a question of guiding the children through the interpretation of the texts. A priest could do it, preferably

13. synoptic Gospels: a book in which the four Gospels are printed side by side for comparison instead of one after another.

textual criticism: a study of the differences found in the ancient manuscripts of the Gospels.

archaeology: a study of the ancient objects found in excavations.

along with an agnostic but serious teacher, one who knows the Gospels as well as the priest does.

While you search for these teachers the limitations of your own culture will float up to the surface. In Florence there are dozens of priests able to give instruction in the Bible at a high level. Men who can read the Greek text with ease and can understand enough of the Hebrew [14] if the need arises.

Can you name a layman thoroughly prepared to face them in discussion? A product of your schools, that is, and not a man from the seminary.

I heard in a lecture given by one of those young intellectuals who have read every book on the face of the earth (except one): 'Gide says if a grain of wheat does not fall to the earth and does not die, it will not bear fruit.'

Now I don't know who this Mr Gide [15] might be, but the Gospels have been my study for years and I shall go on studying them all my life.

The count   Almost anything can be expected from people who have forgotten the Gospels. One can start questioning everything you people teach. One begins to wonder who has made the choices after all.

The truth is that your school began having troubles from birth.

Its date of birth was 1859. A king wanted to enlarge his family possessions. So he began preparations for a war. The first thing he did was to put a general at the head of the government. Next, he sent Parliament out for a holiday. Finally he summoned a count and had him write a law on State education. [16]

14. The oldest part of the Bible is written in Hebrew; the more recent, in Greek.

15. Gide: We found him in the dictionary: a French writer. He probably quoted that sentence from the Gospels in a book of his and the professor believed that it was Gide's own.

16. a king: Victor Emmanuel II.

a general: Alfonso La Marmora.

a holiday: on the occasion of the war Victor Emmanuel dissolved Parliament and took full power himself.

a count: Gabrio Casati. The Casati Law came into existence in 1859. It was not voted upon either by the Piedmontese Parliament or by the subsequent Italian one.

That law, which was imposed by force of arms throughout Italy, is still the backbone of today's school.[17]

History　History was the subject most damaged by this law.

There are several different history surveys. I would like to get the figures on those most in use.

In general they are not history at all. They are narrow-minded, one-sided little tales passed down to the peasants by the conqueror. Italy right in the centre of the world. The losers always bad, the winners all good. There is talk only of kings, generals and stupid wars among nations. The sufferings and struggles of the workers are either ignored or stuck into a corner.

Woe unto the man disliked by generals and armament makers! In the best, most 'modern' book, Gandhi is disposed of in nine lines. Without a word on his thoughts, and even less on his methods.

Civics　Civics is another subject that I know something about, but it does not come up in your schools.

Some teachers say, as an excuse, that it is taught by implication through other subjects. If this were true, it would be too good to believe. If that really is such a great way to teach something, then why don't they use it for all subjects, building a sound structure in which all the elements are blended together and yet can be extracted separately at any time?

Admit that in truth you have hardly any knowledge of civics. You have only a vague notion of what a mayor really is. You have never had dinner in the home of a worker. You don't know the terms of the pending issue on public transport. You only know that the traffic jams are upsetting your private life.

You have never studied these problems, because they scare you. As it also scares you to plunge into the deeper meanings of geography. Your textbook covers all the world but never mentions hunger, monopolies, political systems or racialism.

17. '... in spite of the reform of 1923 and the one of 1930–40 and in spite of the constitutional reorganization of the school after the advent of the Republic, the Casati Law remains the great tissue of which our school is woven at every grade and level' – Luigi Volpicelli.

Comments   One subject is totally missing from your syllabuses: the art of writing.

It is enough simply to see some of the comments you write at the top of your students' compositions. I have a choice collection of them, right here. They are all nothing more than assertions – never a means for improving the work.

'Childish. Infantile. Shows immaturity. Poor. Trivial.' What use can a boy make of this sort of thing? Perhaps he should send his grandfather to school; he's more mature.

Other comments: 'Meagre contents. Poor conception. Pale ideas. No real participation in what you wrote.' The theme must have been wrong, then. It ought not to have been set.

Or: 'Try to improve your form. Incorrect form. Cramped. Unclear. Not well constructed. Poor usage. Try to write more simply. Sentence structure all wrong. Your way of expressing yourself is not always felicitous. You must have better control of your means of expression.' You are the one who should have taught all that. But you don't even believe that writing can be taught; you don't believe there are any objective rules for the art of writing; you are still embalmed in your nineteenth-century individualism.

Then we also meet the creature touched by the hands of gods: 'Spontaneous. Rich flow of ideas. Fitting use of your ideas, in harmony with a striking personality.' Having gone that far, why not just add: 'Blessed be the mother who gave you birth'?

The genius   You returned one of my compositions with a very low grade and this comment: 'Writers are born, not made.' Meanwhile you receive a salary as a teacher of Italian.

The theory of the genius is a bourgeois invention. It was born from a compound of racialism and laziness.

It is also useful in politics. Rather than having to steer through the complex of existing parties, you find it easier to get hold of a de Gaulle, call him a genius and say that *he* is France.

This is the way you operate in your Italian class. Pierino has the gift. I do not. So let's all relax about it.

It doesn't matter whether or not Pierino reflects on his writing. He will write more of those books that already surround him. Five hundred pages that could be reduced to fifty without losing a single idea.

I can learn resignation and go back to the woods.

As for you, you can go on lounging behind your desk and making little marks in your mark book.

School of art   The craft of writing is to be taught like any other craft.

But at Barbiana we had to argue this question among ourselves. One faction wanted to describe the way we go about writing. Others said, 'Art is a serious matter, even if it uses simple techniques. The readers will laugh at us.'

The poor will not laugh at us. The rich can go on laughing all they want, and we shall laugh at them, not able to write either a book or a newspaper with the skill of the poor.

Finally we agreed to write down everything for readers who will love us.

A humble technique   This is the way we do it:

To start with, each of us keeps a notebook in his pocket. Every time an idea comes up, we make a note of it. Each idea on a separate sheet, on one side of the page.

Then one day we gather together all the sheets of paper and spread them on a big table. We look through them, one by one, to get rid of duplications. Next, we make separate piles of the sheets that are related, and these will make up the chapters. Every chapter is sub-divided into small piles, and they will become paragraphs.

At this point we try to give a title to each paragraph. If we can't it means either that the paragraph has no content or that too many things are squeezed into it. Some paragraphs disappear. Some are broken up.

While we name the paragraphs we discuss their logical order, until an outline is born. With the outline set, we reorganize all the piles to follow its pattern.

We take the first pile, spread the sheets on the table, and we find the sequence for them. And so we begin to put down a first draft of the text.

We duplicate that part so that we each can have a copy in

front of us. Then scissors, paste and coloured pencils. We shuffle it all again. New sheets are added. We duplicate again.

A race begins now for all of us to find any word that can be crossed out, any excess adjectives, repetitions, lies, difficult words, over-long sentences and any two concepts that are forced into one sentence.

We call in one outsider after another. We prefer it if they have not had too much school. We ask them to read aloud. And we watch to see if they have understood what we meant to say.

We accept their suggestions if they clarify the text. We reject any suggestions made in the name of caution.

Having done all this hard work and having followed these rules that anyone can use, we often come across an intellectual idiot who announces, 'This letter has a remarkably *personal* style.'

Laziness   Why don't you admit that you don't know what the art of writing is? It is an art that is the very opposite of laziness.

And don't say that you lack the time for it. It would be enough to have one long paper written throughout the year, but written by all the students together.

Speaking of laziness, I can suggest an exercise to amuse your students. Why not spend a year translating Saitta's [18] book into real Italian?

Criminal Trial

You work 210 days a year, of which thirty are lost in giving exams and over thirty more on tests. That leaves only 150 days of school in a year. Half of these school days are lost in oral examinations, which means that there are seventy-five days of teaching against 135 of passing judgement.

Without changing your working contract in the least, you could triple the hours of schooling you give.

Tests in the classroom   While giving a test you used to walk up and down between the rows of desks and see me in trouble and making mistakes, but you never said a word.

18. Saitta : author of a history book.

I have the same situation at home. No one to turn to for help for miles around. No books. No telephone.

Now here I am in 'school'. I came from far away to be taught. Here I don't have to deal with my mother, who promised to be quiet and then interrupted me a hundred times. My sister's little boy is not here to ask me for help with his homework. Here I have silence and good light and a desk all to myself.

And over there, a few steps away, you stand. You know all of these things. You are paid to help me.

Instead, you waste your time keeping me under guard as if I were a thief.

Laziness and terror   You yourself told me that oral examinations are not really school. 'When my class is given the first hour you can take a later train, since I spend the first half-hour on oral exams.'

During those exams the whole class sinks either into laziness or terror. Even the boy being questioned wastes his time. He keeps taking cover, avoids what he understands least, keeps stressing the things he knows well.

To make you happy we need know only how to sell our goods. And how never to keep quiet. And how to fill empty spaces with empty words. To repeat critical remarks read in Sapegno,[19] passing them off as our own and giving the impression that we have read the originals.

Personal opinions   It's even better to air some 'personal opinions'. You hold these personal opinions in high regard: 'In my opinion, Petrarch ...'[20] Perhaps this boy has read two of his poems, perhaps none.

I have heard that in certain American schools whenever the teacher says something, half the students raise their hands and say, 'I agree!' The other half says, 'I don't.' Then they change sides, continuing to chew gum all the while with great energy.

A student who gives personal opinions on things beyond his

19. Sapegno: author of a history of literature. He has read many books. He compares them and criticizes them. Teachers are happy if you repeat what he has written.

20. Petrarch: Italian poet of the fourteenth century.

reach is an imbecile. He should not be praised for it. One goes to school to listen to the teachers.

It can happen on rare occasions that something of our own might be useful to the class or to the teacher. Not just an opinion or something quoted out of a book. Some definite thing seen with our own eyes, at home, in the streets or in the woods.

A clever question   You never asked me questions about such things. On my own, I would never speak out about them. But your young gentlemen could go on asking, with angelic faces, about all sorts of things they already knew. And you would keep encouraging them: 'What a clever question!'

A comedy useless to everyone concerned. Harmful to those bootlickers. Cruel to me, who was unable to be good at that game.

The other dead language

> *Ma ove dorme il furor d'inclite geste*
> *e sien ministri al vivere civile*
> *L'opulenza e il tremore, inutil pompa*
> *e inaugurate immagini dell'Orco*
> *sorgon cippi e marmorei monumenti.*[21]*

'Change into contemporary prose.' My eyes kept wandering over those strange words, not knowing where to come to rest. You smiled to me and whispered, 'Go on, dear; it's so easy. I went through it all yesterday for you. You haven't studied.'

It was true. I hadn't studied. I shall never teach my own students that *'inaugurare'* means *'augurare male'.*† It is already explained in a footnote. But it is a lie. Foscolo made it up because he disliked the poor. He did not want to make an effort on our behalf.

21. A section of 'Sepolcri' by Ugo Foscolo, an Italian poet of the early nineteenth century. This poem might say important things. If the teacher wants us to grasp them, she should simplify the text (with side translation and permission to use the footnotes).

*'But where the furore of illustrious gestures will sleep and luxury and trembling will minister to civic life, Cippi and marble monuments will rise as useless ostentation and ill-omened effigies of the Ogre' (free translation).

†*inaugurare*: to inaugurate; *augurare male*: to forebode.

You asked me to keep a notebook with all those notations, in order to have me learn by heart that curious language of his. I was supposed to learn that language, but where could I ever use it?

For the sake of stretching out a hand to Dick, across all the barriers of language, I was ready to do acrobatics. During work breaks he would sit next to me and make an effort to pronounce 'doulce vita'.* I'd respond with a dirty joke in my worst cockney. And I'd try to make my pronunciation as bad as his. That cockney never used inside an office. That cockney which keeps you among the poor.

Blackmail   Meanwhile the minutes were passing and my mouth would not open. I was sunk in rage and despair.

Those pathetic children couldn't make me out. You have *trained them* since infancy to accept the language of your Monti.† They are already resigned to boredom. They expect nothing else from school.

They would cheer me on with loving sympathy. Like the young people of the St Vincent Charitable Society, they never see the hatred.

No one disliked me. Not even you: 'I'm not going to eat you up.' You sounded so encouraging. You wanted to do your duty by me.

And meanwhile you were destroying every single ideal I had, with the blackmail power of that diploma you have in your hands.

Art   If I had had some time to calm down during those oral examinations (as I now have with my friends while we write these things) I could have convinced you. I'm sure of it. You are not a beast, after all.

At the moment, though, only filthy words and insults kept coming to my mind. Those words that we try hard to hold back while we transform them into arguments.

So, we have understood what art is. It means to dislike some-

---

*'*doulce vita*': English mispronunciation of *La Dolce Vita*, a famous Italian film by Federico Fellini [Translators' note].

† See footnote 11, page 30 [Translators' note].

body or something. To think about it at great length. To have friends help us in patient team work.

Slowly the truth will emerge from beneath the hatred. The work of art is born: a hand held out to your enemy so that he may change.

Infection

After a month at your school I, too, was infected.

During the oral exams my heart would stop beating. I found that I was wishing on others what I did not want done to myself.

I stopped listening to the lessons. I would think only about the oral exams coming up in the next hour.

The best and most exciting subjects – wrapped up and lifeless. As if they had no relationship to the larger world outside. As if they could be confined only to those inches between the blackboard and the teacher's desk.

A worm   At home, I didn't even notice when my mother fell ill. Nor did I have any interest in my neighbours. I never read a newspaper. I couldn't sleep at night.

My mother cried. My father grumbled through his teeth: 'You'd be better off out in the woods.'

I was reduced to studying like a worm.

Until then, I had always had time to approach something as I would if I were teaching it to my pupils. If something seemed important, I would drop the textbook and go deeper into other books to understand it.

After your treatment, I found even the textbook too much. I saw myself underlining the crucial points. Later, my schoolmates suggested even skinnier books for cramming, invented strictly for satisfying your little heads.

Doubts   I reached the point of thinking you were right, and that your culture was the true one. Perhaps we, in our solitude up there, were still dreaming with a simplicity you had left behind centuries ago.

Perhaps our dream of a language that everyone could read, made of plain words, was nothing but a fantasy ahead of its time.

By a hair I missed becoming one of you. Like those children of the poor who change their race when they go up to the university.

The outsider   I did not quite have the time, though, to become as corrupt as you would have liked. In June you gave me a 5 in Italian and a 4 in Latin.

I took the old path through the woods once more and returned to Barbiana. Day after day, from dawn till dark, like a child again.

But I did not pick up the full timetable of the school. Because of the two exams I had to resit, my mentor relieved me from having to teach the younger pupils and from reading the newspaper. I was allowed to study in a room all by myself in order to have silence and the books I did not have at home.

I used to return from the dead only for the reading of letters.

Letters

Alms   Francuccio, from Algeria:

. . . in some places around here the earth is all red and there isn't a blade of grass. Suddenly the train stops. I lean out the window to see what is going on. Three girls with colourful skirts reaching down to their feet. They walk along the train and they don't beg, but people toss them something. They gather it up quickly and hide it in their bosoms. When they have worked their way down to the last carriage, the engineer picks up speed again to thirty kilometres per hour. They tell me that Ben Bella wanted to stop this habit of begging and that Boumédienne, on the other hand, lets it go on. I can't work it out yet. Who is right? What is your opinion, Father?

The language of the poor   Another note from Francuccio:

. . . found a wooden hoop on the street and began tossing it into the air to catch it. I am surrounded by about twenty children, who start to laugh and hold up their hands for me to throw it to them. I do, and we go on for five minutes without a word. All of a sudden the oldest gives a signal to stop. He has noticed my Arabic newspaper. He asks in Arabic what I am doing here and where I came from. We began to talk on the steps of the little mosque. The *muezzin* came up to us and started to talk to me at a great rate. Since I couldn't understand his questions I had to admit that I was not an Arab, but that I could read Arabic. Then he took me into the mosque to read the Koran.[22] He was all excited.

Religion   Sandro, from France:

. . . he stops the car on a side street and asks me to pay him for the ride. I say, '*Machin, je suis catholique,*'[23] and he gives up, but he leaves me stranded right there and I had to walk four kilometres to reach the highway.

Boiled sunflowers   Franco, from Wales:[24]

. . . the priest has a special booklet for confessing foreigners. You say to him, 'I did two sins number twenty-five and I fought off three number twelve.' He gave me a sermon on number twenty-five!

I grow vegetables for a little old lady. Today I had to strip sunflowers all day. She is a vegetarian but would have bought meat just for me. I say no, it's one more experience. So, she picked two sunflower stalks and boiled them for me."

The apolitical girl   Carlo, from Marseilles:[25]

. . . there's a party of Italian students here with a priest. They build barracks for the Algerians at no pay. They don't try to learn French. They don't want to hear about politics. They do a lot of talking about the Vatican Council but make very few strokes with the pickaxe. One of them is a rather stupid girl. Tonight when I went into my room to write to you, she followed me in and threw herself on my bed, saying she was crazy about Florentines.

Praising lies   Edoardo, from London:

. . . it's all the fault of the parents who spoil their children to much. They don't teach them how to spend money, they let them give orders and they treat them like grown men. Parents gain their trust, but is a lie such a bad thing when it can keep a boy away from so many sins? I don't know whether I have made myself clear. True, English children are very sincere. But what does it cost them when

22. mosque: a Muslim church.
muezzin: custodian of the mosque and the initiator of the prayers.
Koran: the sacred book of the Muslims.
23. 'Listen, you, I am a Catholic.'
24. Wales: a region in Great Britain.
25. Marseilles: a city in France.

their mother will never scold them anyway? The parents – what do they gain? If I tell a lie it is a sign that I know what is wrong and I think twice before doing it again.

To our credit   An old union worker from England writes about Paolo:

. . . he is a blessing from God to our factory and a real credit to your school. He is so intense and happy with life. I feel as if God had arranged this thing: you and I so far away from each other and still we think and speak alike. Here many of the workers vote Conservative and read the boss's newspapers, and I tell them, 'I had to wait for this boy to come all the way from Italy to find one who thinks like me. You allow a boy and a Roman Catholic to come and teach you.' [26]

Annibal Caro   When all the letters are read, I shut myself up again with my *Aeneid*.

I read an episode that you like.

Two toughs are disembowelling people while they sleep. List of: people disembowelled, the stolen goods, the names of the men who have given a belt as a gift and the weight of that belt. The whole thing in a stillborn language. [27]

The *Aeneid* was not part of the curriculum. You chose it. I will never forgive you that.

My friends, however, do forgive me. They know that my goal is to be a teacher. But I am just as cut off from things as you are.

Disinfection

Superficial   In September you gave me 4s on both tests. You can't even carry out your chemist's trade very well. Your little scales are not working. How could I know less than I did in June?

You pulled a switch. You switched off a boy. But actually,

26. An international treaty prohibits children under eighteen from working abroad. But labour laws are not broken only in Italy. Children from Barbiana have been able to work in England, Germany, France, Austria, Algeria, Libya. For example, the boys writing these letters were: Francuccio, sixteen; Sandro, fifteen; Franco, fourteen; Carlo, sixteen; Edoardo, sixteen.

27. stillborn: in Italian schools the *Aeneid* is read in the translation of Annibal Caro, a sixteenth-century writer.

without knowing it, you turned on my light. You opened my eyes to you and your culture.

First of all I have found the most accurate insult for defining you: you are simply superficial. You are a society of mutual flatterers that survives because there are so few of you.

Revenge   My father and my brother go off to the woods for me. I cannot take that course again and I do not intend to carry wood on my back, letting the world go on the way it is. That would give you too much satisfaction.

So I was back in Barbiana, and in June I went to take the exam once more.

You failed me again, as if you were spitting on the ground. But I am not going to give up. I will be a teacher and I'll make a better teacher than you.

Second revenge   My other revenge is this letter. We all worked on it together.

Even Gianni did some work. His father is in the hospital. If only Gianni had been as manly last year as he is now. But now it is too late for schooling. They need his apprentice's pay at home. When he heard about this letter, though, he promised to come and help us on Sundays.

He finally came. He read it. He pointed out some words or phrases that were too difficult. He reminded us of some tasty bits of viciousness. He authorized us to make fun of him. He is practically the chief author.

But don't let yourself take comfort from this. You still have to carry him around in your soul. He can't yet express himself.

Waiting for an answer   Now we are here awaiting an answer. There must be someone in some *magistrale* who will write to us:

Dear boys,
Not all teachers are like that lady of yours. Don't become racialists yourselves.

Although I can't agree with everything you say, I know that our school isn't good enough. Only a perfect school can afford to refuse new people and new cultures. And there is no perfect school. Neither yours nor ours.

However, if any of you who want to be teachers will come and take your examinations here, I have a group of colleagues ready to shut their eyes for your sake.

In pedagogy, we shall ask you only about Gianni. In literature, we shall ask how you wrote this beautiful letter. In Latin, some old words your grandfather still uses. In geography, the customs of English farmers. In history, the reasons why mountain people come down to the plains. In science, you can tell us about *sormenti* and give us the correct name of the tree that bears cherries.

We are waiting for this letter. We know it will come.

Our address* is : Scuola di Barbiana,
                Vicchio Mugello,
                Firenze, Italy.

* New address : Ragazzi di Barbiana, Via del Colle 51, Calenzano-Firenze, Italy [Translators' note].

Part 3
Documentation

In Part 3 we have gathered the statistical tables that are not strictly necessary for understanding the text.

They will be useful to any friend who wants to deepen his understanding and to the not-so-good friend who does not trust us.

Notes for Table A

The figures in roman type inside the rectangles represent the enrolled students; the figures in italics with an 'R', the repeaters.

Under the rectangles the roman-type figures with a 'p' represent the promoted. The figures in italics with an 'f' are the failures, those with 'd' the dropouts; 'e' indicates elementary, (i) intermediate.

In this table (unlike Table C) the figures for the repeaters are the official ones.

The 'born' and the 'dead' are taken from the *Annuari Statistici Italiana 1949–57* [Yearbooks of Italian Statistics 1949–57]. The schools' data up to 1963–4 are from the *Annuari Statistici dell'Istruzione Italiana 1956–65*.

Some of the data for 1964–5 are from the *Compendio Statistico Italiano 1966* [Italian Statistical Compendium 1966].

At this date – March 1967 – when we are delivering the manuscript of this book, the *Annuario Statistico dell'Istruzione Italiana 1966* has not yet been published. We were able, however, to glance through it, courtesy of some friends.

The *Annuari Statistici dell'Istruzione Italiana* appear every year. The volume for 1963, however, was not published. The next year a single volume for 1963–4 was published. This volume lacks some important data (first and second intermediate students for 1960–61 and 1961–2).

Courtesy of the general manager of ISTAT [Central Institute of Statistics] we have the honour of printing these data never published before.

The official data on schools are published after great delay. For instance, the *Annuario* for 1965, which was released in March 1966, carries only the 1963–4 data for the enrolled and the repeaters, and the 1963–4 data for the students passed or failed. The same is true for the preceding years.

What is surprising is the large number of children who drop out during the school year (i.e. the difference between the number of enrolled students and the number who are listed as promoted or failed at the end of the school year).

We have been offered this explanation: some school principals or superintendents artificially swell the roll in order to avoid elimination of sections or to obtain a larger number of teachers.

The intention of these public servants might be good, but it is their fault if the official figures of the enrolled children are not very reliable.

The damage done to our computation of the lost children is unimportant. This number stays the same. Rather, the date of the loss must be anticipated.

The Minister of Education presented to the Parliament in 1965 the largest budget of all Cabinets: 17,773 thousand million lire (more than 20 per cent of all the government expenditures). We have seen in our notes how well informed the Minister is on the conditions of the schools. Should a Member of Parliament ask, he could never tell how many children there are in the school system.

The newspapers usually publish in October the number of enrolled students, and in July the number of those promoted or failed. They write long articles embroidering on this subject.

It would be fun to find out if they make up those figures, or if this is done for them by some employee in the Ministry.

Table A

Born in 1948: 1,000,000 — Dead 80,000 — Survivors 920,000

	Survivors	
Ie54-5	1,180,000	258,000 R
857,000 p	225,000 f	98,000 d
IIe55-6	1,050,000	161,000 R
851,000 p	155,000 f	47,000 d
IIIe56-7	1,021,000	143,000 R
817,000 p	109,000 f	95,000 d
IVe57-8	928,000	73,000 R
846,000 p	40,000 f	42,000 d
Ve58-9	870,000	34,000 R
790,000 p	50,000 f	30,000 d
Ii59-60	577,000	82,000 R
398,000 p	156,000 f	23,000 d
IIi60-61	463,000	65,000 R
394,000 p	109,000 f	14,000 d
IIIi61-2	408,000	33,000 R
359,000 p		

Born in 1949: 940,000 — Dead 68,000 — Survivors 872,000

	Survivors	
Ie55-6	1,128,000	256,000 R
874,000 p	166,000 f	88,000 d
IIe56-7	1,056,000	151,000 R
835,000 p	135,000 f	86,000 d
IIIe57-8	1,003,000	118,000 R
835,000 p	104,000 f	64,000 d
IVe58-9	888,000	42,000 R
816,000 p	39,000 f	33,000 d
Ve59-60	857,000	45,000 R
768,000 p	56,000 f	30,000 d
Ii60-61	598,000	89,000 R
408,000 p	159,000 f	31,000 d
IIi61-2	488,000	67,000 R
365,000 p	109,000 f	14,000 d
IIIi62-3	410,000	38,000 R
389,000 p	56,000 f	

Born in 1950: 908,000 — Dead 59,000 — Survivors 849,000

	Survivors	
Ie56-7	1,050,000	201,000 R
809,000 p	128,000 f	113,000 d
IIe57-8	1,006,000	141,000 R
840,000 p	102,000 f	64,000 d
IIIe58-9	984,000	113,000 R
886,000 p	48,000 f	50,000 d
IVe59-60	923,000	40,000 R
814,000 p	69,000 f	40,000 d
Ve60-61	861,000	53,000 R
725,000 p	98,000 f	37,000 d
Ii61-2	664,000	89,000 R
433,000 p	183,000 f	48,000 d
IIi62-3	516,000	72,000 R
396,000 p	106,000 f	14,000 d
IIIi63-4	438,000	35,000 R
415,000 p	59,000 f	

Born in 1951: 861,000 — Dead 57,000 — Survivors 804,000

	Survivors	
Ie57-8	958,000	168,000 R
810,000 p	76,000 f	72,000 d
IIe58-9	968,000	122,000 R
793,000 p	107,000 f	68,000 d
IIIe59-60	875,000	62,000 R
762,000 p	67,000 f	46,000 d
IVe60-61	852,000	62,000 R
725,000 p	82,000 f	45,000 d
Ve61-2	847,000	93,000 R
695,000 p	89,000 f	63,000 d
Ii62-3	668,000	111,000 R
452,000 p	178,000 f	38,000 d
IIi63-4	531,000	72,000 R
408,000 p	101,000 f	22,000 d
IIIi64-5	459,000	36,000 R

Table A (continued)

Born in 1952 860,000
Dead 56,000
Survivors 804,000

Ie58–9	897,000	113,000 R
762,000 p	75,000 f	60,000 d
IIe59–60	895,000	124,000 R
755,000 p	104,000 f	36,000 d
IIIe60–61	841,000	67,000 R
722,000 p	81,000 f	38,000 d
IVe61–2	839,000	83,000 R
703,000 p	87,000 f	49,000 d
Ve62–3	800,000	87,000 R
680,000 p	90,000 f	30,000 d
Ii63–4	716,000	112,000 R
514,000 p	115,000 f	47,000 d
IIi64–5	590,000	65,000 R
IIIi65–6	472,000	28,000 R

Born in 1953 864,000
Dead 49,000
Survivors 815,000

Ie59–60	874,000	90,001 R
746,000 p	79,000	49,000 d
IIe60–61	895,000	118,000 R
740,000 p	101,000 f	54,000 d
IIIe61–2	847,000	84,000 d
722,000 p	85,000	40,000 d
IVe62–3	826,000	85,000 R
705,000 p	91,000 f	30,000 d
Ve63–4	793,000	83,000 R
685,000 p	88,000 f	20,000 d
Ii64–5	683,000	98,000 R

Born in 1954 860,000
Dead 46,000
Survivors 814,000

Ie60–61	890,000	99,000 R
758,000 p	91,000 f	41,000 d
IIe61–2	915,000	121,000 R
756,000 p	110,000 f	49,000 d
IIIe62–3	862,000	90,000 d
743,000 p	89,000 f	30,000 d
IVe63–4	844,000	86,000 d
722,000 p	96,000 f	36,000 d
Ve64–5	809,000	81,000 R

Born in 1955 869,000
Dead 43,000
Survivors 826,000

Ie61–2	906,000	115,000 R
762,000 p	101,000 f	43,000 d
IIe62–3	917,000	123,000 R
770,000 p	102,000 f	45,000 d
IIIe63–4	879,000	92,000 d
756,000 p	95,000 f	28,000 d
IVe64–5	859,000	89,000 R

Table B

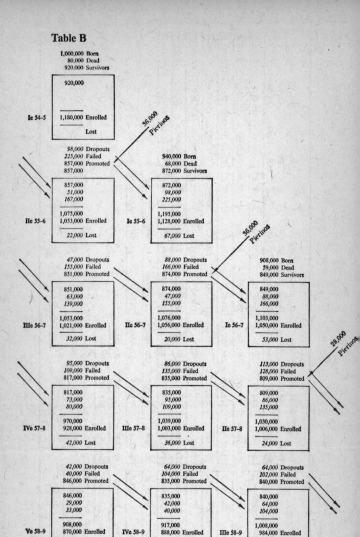

1,000,000 Born
80,000 Dead
920,000 Survivors

920,000

Ic 54–5   1,180,000 Enrolled

       Lost

36,000 Piertinos

98,000 Dropouts
225,000 Failed
857,000 Promoted
857,000

940,000 Born
68,000 Dead
872,000 Survivors

857,000
51,000
167,000

872,000
98,000
225,000

1,075,000
IIc 55–6   1,053,000 Enrolled

   22,000 Lost

1,195,000
Ic 55–6   1,128,000 Enrolled

   67,000 Lost

36,000 Piertinos

47,000 Dropouts
155,000 Failed
851,000 Promoted

88,000 Dropouts
166,000 Failed
874,000 Promoted

908,000 Born
59,000 Dead
849,000 Survivors

851,000
63,000
139,000

874,000
47,000
155,000

849,000
88,000
166,000

1,053,000
IIIc 56–7   1,021,000 Enrolled

   32,000 Lost

1,076,000
IIc 56–7   1,056,000 Enrolled

   20,000 Lost

1,103,000
Ic 56–7   1,050,000 Enrolled

   53,000 Lost

28,000 Piertinos

95,000 Dropouts
109,000 Failed
817,000 Promoted

86,000 Dropouts
135,000 Failed
835,000 Promoted

113,000 Dropouts
128,000 Failed
809,000 Promoted

817,000
73,000
80,000

835,000
95,000
109,000

809,000
86,000
135,000

970,000
IVc 57–8   928,000 Enrolled

   42,000 Lost

1,039,000
IIIc 57–8   1,003,000 Enrolled

   36,000 Lost

1,030,000
IIc 57–8   1,006,000 Enrolled

   24,000 Lost

42,000 Dropouts
40,000 Failed
846,000 Promoted

64,000 Dropouts
104,000 Failed
835,000 Promoted

64,000 Dropouts
102,000 Failed
840,000 Promoted

846,000
29,000
33,000

835,000
42,000
40,000

840,000
64,000
104,000

908,000
Vc 58–9   870,000 Enrolled

   38,000 Lost

917,000
IVc 58–9   888,000 Enrolled

   29,000 Lost

1,008,000
IIIc 58–9   984,000 Enrolled

   24,000 Lost

*Notes for Table B follow on page 122.

Table B (continued)

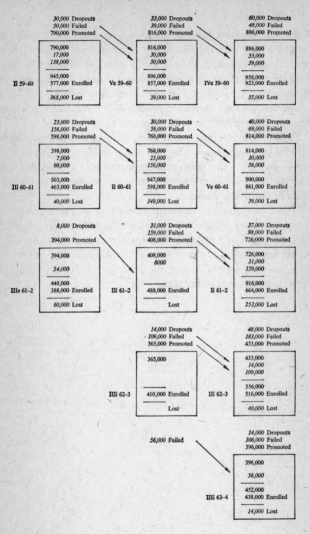

Notes for Table B

This table explains how we computed the theoretical composition of a class and the number of students lost. It would have been nice to extend it at least to the group of children born in 1952, in order to compare the selection made by the new and the old intermediate schools. For lack of sufficient data on the recent school years, we are obliged to publish only three columns (representing children born in 1948, 1949 and 1950).

Each rectangle represents a class. The arrows indicate where the children come from. The sum of the children carried over by the arrows gives the theoretical composition of a class. By subtracting the number of enrolled children we obtain the number of those lost to the school.

Those lost children represent (according to the rectangle in which they are written) the boys mentioned on page 38 under the heading 'lost earnings'. The teacher of that class does not know them and is not responsible for their loss. She is responsible, instead, for the loss of the students seen in the rectangle directly to the right of her class.

Notes for Table C

Our figures in the text, from pages 36 to 53, are a reduction in the scale of 1 to 29,900 of the figures in Table C (children born in 1951).

The figures in italics are estimates.

The figures of the enrolled and of the promoted reproduce the data of ISTAT. Those who dropped out, failed and were lost to the class are easily calculated from the ISTAT data.

The ISTAT data for the repeaters were totally useless. The Ministry of Education also regards as repeaters the children who drop out of school after 15 March, but does not say what portion of the total they represent. We, then, prefer our data computed on the hypothesis (likely indeed) that all those promoted will continue their studies. We obtained these data by subtracting the promoted from the number of enrolled children in the following school year.

Were our hypothesis not true, the number of children lost to the school would be even greater than we claim.

However, this is not valid for the fifth elementary year. In this year the number of children lost to the school is larger than that of the failed. This shows that many of the fifth-year children who are promoted do not continue their studies.

In this table the teacher is directly responsible for the lost. A good teacher, however, should also care for the lost children mentioned in Table B, that is, the children who should be in his class as repeaters and have, perhaps, been mentioned to him by his colleague who failed them.

If we had added the lost children of Table B to those of Table C and reminded the teacher about all of them, our action would not have been absurd. They are not, in fact, the same children. We did not add them simply in order to keep the text and the tables parallel. In statistical tables a boy must be counted only once even though he was lost by two teachers.

Table C Follow-up of Children Born in 1950

Year	Date	Make-up of class		Outcome			Lost	
		Enrolled	Repeaters	Dropouts	Failed	Promoted	to the year	to the school
I Elementary	October 1956 June 1957	1,050,000	201,000	147,000	128,000	809,000		
II Elementary	October 1957 June 1958	1,006,000	197,000	64,000	102,000	840,000	275,000	121,000
III Elementary	October 1958 June 1959	984,000	144,000	60,000	48,000	886,000	166,000	8,000
IV Elementary	October 1959 June 1960	923,000	37,000	40,000	69,000	814,000	98,000	16,000
V Elementary	October 1960 June 1961	861,000	47,000	37,000	98,000	726,000	109,000	19,000
I Intermediate	October 1961 June 1962	664,000	119,000	48,000	183,000	433,000	316,000	194,000
II Intermediate	October 1962 June 1963	516,000	83,000	14,000	106,000	396,000	231,000	132,000
III Intermediate	October 1963 June 1964	438,000	42,000	—	59,000	415,000	120,000	41,000
Total	October 1956 June 1964						1,315,000	531,000

Table C (continued)

Year	Date	Make-up of class		Outcome			Lost	
		Enrolled	Repeaters	Dropouts	Failed	Promoted	to the year	to the school
I Elementary	October 1957 June 1958	958,000	154,000	105,000	76,000	810,000	181,000	88,000
II Elementary	October 1958 June 1959	968,000	158,000	68,000	107,000	793,000	175,000	42,000
III Elementary	October 1959 June 1960	875,000	82,000	46,000	67,000	762,000	113,000	27,000
IV Elementary	October 1960 June 1961	852,000	90,000	45,000	82,000	725,000	127,000	10,000
V Elementary	October 1961 June 1962	847,000	122,000	63,000	89,000	695,000	278,000	181,000
I Intermediate	October 1962 June 1963	668,000	99,000	38,000	178,000	452,000	216,000	70,000
II Intermediate	October 1963 June 1964	531,000	79,000	22,000	101,000	408,000	123,000	47,000
III Intermediate	October 1964 June 1965	459,000	51,000		42,000	436,000		
Total	October 1957 June 1965						1,213,000	465,000

Table C (continued)

Year	Date	Make-up of class		Outcome			Lost to the year	Lost to the school
		Enrolled	Repeaters	Dropouts	Failed	Promoted		
I Elementary	October 1958 June 1959	897,000	93,000	91,000	75,000	762,000		107,000
II Elementary	October 1959 June 1960	895,000	133,000	36,000	104,000	755,000	166,000	
III Elementary	October 1960 June 1961	841,000	86,000	38,000	81,000	722,000	140,000	
IV Elementary	October 1961 June 1962	839,000	117,000	49,000	87,000	703,000	119,000	12,000
V Elementary	October 1962 June 1963	800,000	97,000	30,000	90,000	680,000	136,000	32,000
I Intermediate	October 1963 June 1964	716,000	146,000	47,000	155,000	514,000	230,000	142,000
II Intermediate	October 1964 June 1965	590,000	76,000	13,000	111,000	466,000	202,000	90,000
III Intermediate	October 1965 June 1966	472,000	18,000		41,000	443,000	124,000	61,000
Total	October 1958 June 1966						1,117,000	444,000

Notes for Table D

Figure 7 on page 52 is based on Table D. But in this table one can single out each particular boy. Each one is marked with a number. For instance, the number 6 in italics represents a Pierino (see page 39).

The figures from 1 to 32 represent the children who have been assigned to the teacher in a first elementary year class (without consideration of their being repeaters or not).

The figures in italics represent the children added to the class later (repeaters and Pierino).

The number of children in each of the three columns corresponds to the data from Table C for the year 1951, reduced by the factor 1 : 29,900.

Table D

First elementary year
1 2 3 4 5 6 7 8 9 10 11 12 13 14 15 16 17 18 19 20 21 22 23 24 25 26 27 28 29 30 31 32

Second
1 2 3 4 5 1 2 3 4 5 6 7 8 9 10 11 12 13 14 15 16 17 18 19 20 21 22 23 24 25 26 6

Third
2 3 4 5 7 8 9 1 2 3 4 5 6 7 8 9 10 11 12 13 14 15 16 17 18 19 20 21 6

Second 22 23 24 25 26 27 28 29 30

To work *I* 31 32

Fourth
4 5 7 8 9 10 11 12 1 2 3 4 5 6 7 8 9 10 11 12 13 14 15 16 17 18 19 6

Third 2 20 21 22 23 24 25 26 27 28 29 30

I 3 31 32

Fifth
9 10 11 12 13 14 15 16 1 2 3 4 5 6 7 8 9 10 11 12 13 14 15 16 17 18 19 6

Fourth 2 4 5 8 20 21 22 23 24 25 26 27 28 29 30

I 3 7 31 32

First intermediate year
14 15 16 17 18 19 1 2 3 4 5 6 7 8 9 10 11 12 13 14 15 6

Fifth 2 4 5 8 9 18 19 20 21 22 23 24 25 26 27 28 29 30

I 3 7 10 11 12 13 16 17 31 32

Second
18 19 20 21 22 1 2 3 4 5 6 7 8 9 10 11 6

First 2 4 5 8 9 14 13 14 15 18 19 20 21 22 23 24 25 26 27 28 29 30

I 3 7 10 11 12 13 15 16 17 16 17 31 32

Third
21 22 23 24 1 2 3 4 5 6 7 8 9 10 11 6

Second 2 4 5 8 9 14 19 11 12 13 14 15 18 19 20 21 22 23 24 25 26 27 28 29 30

I 3 7 10 11 12 13 15 16 17 18 20 16 17 31 32

Notes for Table E

The data for this table are taken from Table 5, A and B, of the book *Distribution by Age of the Pupils of Elementary and Intermediate Schools*, I S T A T, *1963*.

The age of the boys as of 31 December 1959 is indicated.

We could not find out who the 14,191 children were who were not yet six years old on 31 December.

Only children born on 1 January (about 2,000) could have been legally enrolled.

The number of Pierinos can be obtained by subtracting the mysterious 14,191 from the 45,718 children expected in the second year.

Table E

Age	Elementary					Intermediate			Upper school					Total
	1	2	3	4	5	1	2	3	1	2	3	4	5	
						Actual figures								
5	14,191	—	—	—	—	—	—	—	—	—	—	—	—	14,191
6	713,404	45,718	—	—	—	—	—	—	—	—	—	—	—	759,122
7	106,699	613,889	47,282	—	—	—	—	—	—	—	—	—	—	767,870
8	29,099	161,345	538,985	43,209	—	—	—	—	—	—	—	—	—	773,448
9	12,231	65,547	171,881	517,438	43,030	—	—	—	—	—	—	—	—	810,127
10	4,886	26,569	75,355	199,689	454,737	42,791	—	—	—	—	—	—	—	804,027
11	2,532	12,833	35,528	102,577	209,748	325,123	35,850	—	—	—	—	—	—	724,191
12	1,144	5,052	14,675	43,069	97,775	182,580	205,408	30,237	382	—	—	—	—	580,322
13	525	1,871	5,534	15,157	40,162	82,715	130,350	153,945	23,453	382	—	—	—	454,094
14	143	397	1,039	2,432	6,497	18,083	44,784	74,265	69,923	15,499	248	—	—	233,310
15	—	—	—	—	—	4,932	15,266	38,476	49,398	54,307	12,918	242	—	175,539
16	—	—	—	—	—	1,849	4,722	15,444	29,348	43,719	44,261	13,062	162	152,567
17	—	—	—	—	—	986	1,474	5,267	13,398	26,951	31,993	35,730	10,572	126,371
18	—	—	—	—	—	552	562	1,747	5,602	12,978	19,802	27,124	25,666	94,033
19	—	—	—	—	—	547	281	841	2,779	6,500	11,305	19,376	21,556	63,188
20	—	—	—	—	—	380	163	578	1,157	2,511	4,974	10,237	14,137	34,137
21+	—	—	—	—	—	469	148	476	1,560	2,490	3,987	9,262	15,337	33,729

Table E (continued)

Age	Elementary					Intermediate			Upper school					Total
	1	2	3	4	5	1	2	3	1	2	3	4	5	
	Percentage of students in each year													
5	1.7	—	—	—	—	—	—	—	—	—	—	—	—	0.2
6	79.5	5.1	—	—	—	—	—	—	—	—	—	—	—	11.5
7	12.5	63.7	5.3	—	—	—	—	—	—	—	—	—	—	11.6
8	3.6	17.0	60.5	4.7	—	—	—	—	—	—	—	—	—	11.7
9	1.5	7.6	19.3	56.0	5.0	—	—	—	—	—	—	—	—	12.3
10	0.6	3.2	8.5	21.6	53.4	6.5	—	—	—	—	—	—	—	12.2
11	0.3	1.6	4.0	11.1	24.6	49.2	8.2	—	—	—	—	—	—	11.0
12	0.2	0.6	1.7	4.7	11.5	27.6	46.8	9.4	0.2	—	—	—	—	8.8
13	0.1	0.3	0.6	1.6	4.7	12.5	29.7	47.9	11.9	0.2	—	—	—	6.9
14	—	—	0.1	0.3	0.8	2.7	10.2	23.1	35.5	9.4	0.2	—	—	3.5
15	—	—	—	—	—	0.7	3.5	12.0	25.1	32.9	10.0	0.2	—	2.7
16	—	—	—	—	—	0.3	1.1	4.8	14.9	26.4	34.2	11.4	0.2	2.3
17	—	—	—	—	—	0.1	0.3	1.6	6.8	16.3	24.7	31.1	12.1	1.9
18	—	—	—	—	—	0.1	0.1	0.5	2.8	7.9	15.3	23.6	29.4	1.4
19	—	—	—	—	—	0.1	0.1	0.3	1.4	3.9	8.7	16.8	24.6	1.0
20	—	—	—	—	—	0.1	—	0.2	0.6	1.5	3.8	8.9	16.2	0.5
21+	—	—	—	—	—	0.1	—	0.2	0.8	1.5	3.1	8.0	17.5	0.5

Table F Slaughter of the Older

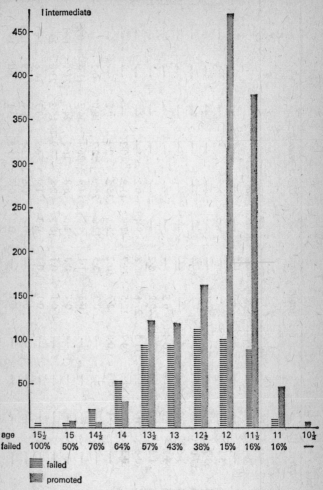

age	15½	15	14½	14	13½	13	12½	12	11½	11	10½
failed	100%	50%	76%	64%	57%	43%	38%	15%	16%	16%	—

failed

promoted

* Notes for Table F follow on page 134.

Table F (continued)

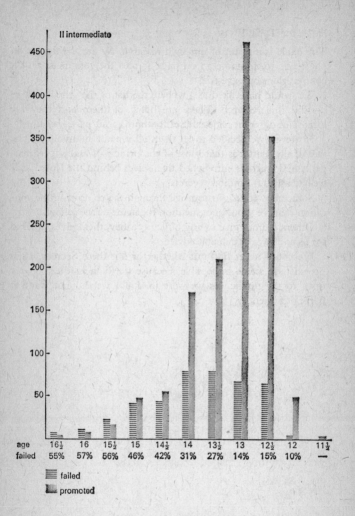

II intermediate

age	16½	16	15½	15	14½	14	13½	13	12½	12	11½
failed	55%	57%	56%	46%	42%	31%	27%	14%	15%	10%	—

▤ failed
▨ promoted

Notes for Table F

This table is a result of our own research. So are the figures on pages 42, 50, footnote 37 on page 45 and the comments on the compositions on page 102.

We would have liked to give here the list of the schools where we did this research. There are many of them and they are located in different regions. (See footnote 42 on page 47.)

However, we decided to let them all remain anonymous. The fact of the matter is that some of the principals and superintendents and teachers entrenched themselves behind the Rules, as if we had asked for military secrets.

Some allowed us to rummage through the records on the condition that we should not mention the name of the school.

Others did not give us any difficulty; they, themselves, worked for us and gave us valuable advice.

We could never find out whether or not these Secrecy Rules do exist. It seems impossible, because the data in question are open to the public. As we were in doubt we did not want to harm our friends.

Dear School of Barbiana

Let me first introduce myself. I am a former member of the British House of Commons, and a former Minister of Education. For nearly ten years, altogether, I used to speak on education in the British Parliament as an official spokesman of my political party. Now I have left politics, and I am about to become Vice-Chancellor of Leeds University, a large university in the north of England.

I have been greatly impressed by your *Letter*, and want to send you a reply of my own. I notice, first, that your *Letter* expresses passionately, even angrily, a belief which cannot be too often or too strongly reaffirmed: *far too many boys and girls, in your country and in mine, are still being allowed to write themselves off well below their true potential*. This is one of the most important truths about the world today, and I have always tried to do what I could to bring it to people's attention. It is the lesson taught by all the major reports on education which have appeared in my country during the last twelve years – Crowther, Robbins, Newsom and Plowden. But I think your *Letter to a Teacher* drives it home best of all.

My second reason for sending you this reply is that I was particularly interested in what you had to say about Pierino – the professional-class child who goes straight into a higher form – as well as about Gianni, the child of poor parents who needs more 'full-time' education most. I think you are right to point out the educational deprivation which Pierino suffers through being so cut off from the culture of Gianni. The education of a favoured minority must be less effective, simply as education, if it affords them no opportunity for close contact with children who may not have heard of Cicero but who – as you vividly express it – 'can read the sounds of their valley for miles around'. Highly selective schooling, in your own words, 'deprives the poor of the means of expressing themselves. It [also] deprives the rich of a knowledge of things as they are.' I personally found it salutary to have the case against a rigidly selective system made so force-fully in this way.

My third reason for writing is simply the desire to congratulate you on the sheer quality and effectiveness of your *Letter* as a piece of writing. You are of course concerned with better schooling, and not with literary elegance. But the vividness and precision of your language matches the clarity of your thought. And for all the sting of your polemic, you take up no positions that you are not prepared to defend with reasoned argument and rigorous analysis.

There are many points I wish I could discuss with you. I am glad you devote a number of pages to the *content* of secondary education – what we really mean when we speak of 'secondary education for all'. Your statistical analysis of failure in the Italian schools, and the diagrams which accompany and illustrate it, are achievements which not only merited the prize exceptionally awarded by the Italian Physical Society, but also help to justify what I and many others have said about offering all children the opportunity to learn something about modern numerate techniques. No one who really wants to try and understand the workings of our society can afford to ignore what a Professor of Economics in my country has called 'the immense gains to be derived from access to the principal technique of analytical thinking developed by man'.

I hope you might be pleasantly surprised by the number of schools in Britain where you would find considerable sympathy with your ideas. For instance, I think most of our teachers, and certainly those teaching in country schools, *would* be interested to hear about *sormenti*, or the correct name of the tree that bears cherries. Many of them have described to me how valuable visits abroad are in encouraging boys and girls to make progress in the use of a second language. Many, again, would strongly endorse your view that if you want good English – or Italian – prose composition, you must get people to write about experiences that are real to them. As for history, schools in my country do not have nearly enough money to spend on books, but I should judge that few history books for schools would nowadays make the mistake of dismissing Gandhi in a few lines – and, if they did, even fewer teachers would wish to buy them.

I found myself particularly intrigued by one sentence in the *Letter*: 'A man can call himself a teacher when he has no cultural interests just for his own sake.' My own inclination is to feel that there are 'goods of solitude' as well as 'goods of society' – and I do not see why a teacher, provided that (as you rightly insist) he works hard at his job, should not enjoy his own cultural interests in his spare time, just like anyone else. Some of us do like to spend a small part of the day alone if we can, and I thought you were too hard on the girl in your class who likes to shut herself in her room to listen to Bach. However, I think there is an important truth contained in your statement that 'knowledge is only meant to be passed on', since it reminds one that teacher-training is ultimately concerned with *what one can pass on to children*, rather than with academic study as such.

Your letter is full of flashes of insight which I found exciting and sometimes highly disturbing. 'Whenever you speak to a worker you manage to get it all wrong: your choice of words, your tone, your jokes.' As someone who started life as a Pierino, I accept the justice of this comment, except that I usually have the sense not to attempt the jokes. Of course this difficulty of communication does not only apply vertically in our present-day society, to communication between the salaried classes and the wage-earners; it can apply equally, to take an example from my own country, to communication between a leader-writer on a sophisticated London weekly and a supporter of Mr Enoch Powell in the West Midlands.

Most striking of all is your comment on Stokely Carmichael at his last trial, declaring that 'There isn't a white man I can trust.' 'If the young white man [who had given his entire life to the cause of the blacks] took offence at what Carmichael said, then Carmichael is right. If he is truly with the blacks, the young man must swallow it, draw aside and keep on loving.' Here I am with you completely – in fact it was this comment, more than anything else, that made me want to write to you. Where race relations are concerned, it seems to me quite crucial that one's commitment should not be dictated by a woolly belief in 'tolerance', by charity or by a desire to be commended as a 'white liberal'. If it matters to us that our society should become a *juster* society for all (not just a more tolerant society), then we will do what we can irrespective of what other people – be they black or white – may choose to say of us.

You have written an angry *Letter*, but it is a *Letter* which stands for maturity as against triviality, and recognizes the gains we could all share from an educational system which more effectively lowers the barriers to civilized human intercourse. And for all the biting tone of your *Letter*, you end on a note of expectancy and hope – the hope that someone in authority will recognize in reply that 'There is no perfect school. Neither yours nor ours.' Of course this 'someone', if he is a real person, will almost certainly have started life not as Gianni but as Pierino a Pierino who has himself come to recognize the defects in his own education. It is a fitting ending to your fine *Letter* that you are prepared to listen to him when he admonishes you: 'Don't become racialists yourselves.'

Yours sincerely
Edward Boyle

Other Penguin Education Specials

Death at an Early Age

Jonathan Kozol

The destruction of the hearts and minds of Negro children in the
Boston public schools.

The discrimination that has made second-class citizens of one
generation of coloured adults will as surely disinherit their children,
future British citizens now in our classrooms, unless we urgently
root out from ourselves – parents, neighbours, teachers,
administrators – and from our teaching, our school books, our
assumptions about language and thinking the subtle prejudices that,
with a multitude of small cuts, wound the heart and mind. *Death at
an Early Age* is a moving personal testament from America: it also
carries an urgent message for our society. Time for action may be
passing faster than we think.

State School

R. F. Mackenzie

When he became headmaster of a secondary modern school in the
Scottish coalfields, R. F. Mackenzie found himself in charge of
children whose lives promised to become as derelict as their
surroundings – unhappy, delinquent, their futures blocked by a
joyless and, to them, impossible tradition of academic education.

This anthology of extracts from his writings describes his fight to
provide them with an education which was both imaginative and
relevant. Trips in the Scottish countryside, which were the
children's first experience of independence and of the beauty of the
land they lived in, convinced him that the school should acquire a
permanent base in the Highlands, an ambition which thrust him
into a long and bitter struggle with an officialdom which prized
narrow restrictions more than such dreams. There were other dreams,
too, and other defeats : staff who betrayed his ideal of a school free
from authoritarian modes of discipline, delinquent children who
tried, unsuccessfully, to keep out of trouble. But these pages speak of
anything but defeat : they describe the authentic feel of the
experience which education should provide, especially for the
underprivileged, and demonstrate convincingly how good the victory
will be when it is, finally, won.

R. F. Mackenzie is now headmaster of Summerhill Comprehensive
School in Aberdeen.

The School That I'd Like

Edited by Edward Blishen

In all the millions of words that are written annually about education, one vewpoint is invariably absent – that of the child, the client of the school. It is difficult to think of another sphere of social activity in which the opinions of the customer are so persistently overlooked.

In December 1957 the *Observer* organized a competition for secondary school children to remedy this, and invited essays on 'The school that I'd like'. We publish a selection of the entries here. They constitute a passionate and sustained attack upon our present educational order. Their intelligence and originality are only rivalled by their unanimity. The writers demand to be allowed to think, to encounter head-on the raw material of learning, to be at risk, to escape from boredom into the joy of discovery, to be *partners* in their education. No one will read this selection without feeling some shame at what we have done to these children. Who will answer them? Who will explain to them why they should not have what they demand?

'I am tired of hearing that the hope of my country lies in my generation. If you give me the same indoctrination . . . how can you expect me to be any different from you?' *15-year-old girl*

'The essays are remarkably articulate. . . . This is a stimulating and challenging book.' *Teaching*

Children in Distress

Alec Clegg and Barbara Megson

Two out of every hundred children have to be given direct help by the State – whether it be psychiatric, social or medical. But are these the only children 'in distress'? What about those children who do not qualify for State help?

Alec Clegg and Barbara Megson estimate that perhaps 12 per cent of our children desperately need help, but do not qualify to receive it. *Children in Distress* paints an agonizing picture of child distress, based on the authors' long experience in educational administration. They argue that it is the schools – in daily contact with the children – that are the agencies best suited to help this large and saddening section of our child population.

'. . . this book, containing a wealth of information and ideas based on the experience of very many schools, can help teachers who want to help their problem pupils, but just do not know how to start. It can help them, probably, more than any other single volume.' *The Times Educational Supplement*

Education for Democracy

Edited by David Rubenstein and Colin Stoneman

The time for a radical manifesto on British education is long overdue. For over twenty-five years the struggle to democratize our system has been held back by those who see the proper function of education as the production of an elite and, as the most efficient means of effecting this, the labelling of children as A's or D's at the earliest possible opportunity. Those children who do not meet the requirements of the current elite have had some reason to be disconsolate about their fate.

Here at last – appropriately at a time when the 'backlash' is receiving all the attention, if not actually gaining the upper hand – is a bold definition of the nature and purpose of 'education for democracy'.

The contributors to this collection, all of whom have to grapple daily with these problems on the lecture-hall or classroom floor, do not attempt to put forward a single, easy solution. But whether they are writing about the content of the primary curriculum or university examinations, about slum schools or the new technology of learning, there is one fundamental belief which they all hold in common. They demand an education system which cares about *all* children, regardless of race, class or intelligence, and which helps to build a democratic society by upholding the qualities of compassion and respect within its own walls.

'This is a thought-provoking and stimulating book which raises the question as to what education for democracy should be.' *Tribune*

**Neill and Summerhill
A Man and his Work**

A Pictorial Study by John Walmsley

A. S. Neill is the most famous schoolmaster in the world. What he has succeeded in doing at his school, Summerhill, has been perhaps the most important single reason for our increasing respect for school children as individuals.

This remarkable collection of photographs and reminiscences is a tribute to this man and his work. We once asked John Walmsley, the photographer, why it included so few pictures of Neill himself. 'The children,' he replied, 'are pictures of Neill.'

'Walmsley's pictures and the reminiscences of a score of friendly contributors provide a refreshingly uncultish testimony to the life-work of a humane educator.' *New Society*